PhD by Published Work

Palgrave Research Skills

Palgrave Teaching and Learning

Series Editor: Sally Brown

Further titles are in preparation

PhD by Published Work

A Practical Guide for Success

Susan Smith
Head of Curriculum Development and Review
Leeds Beckett University, UK

 macmillan
education   palgrave

First published 2015 by
PALGRAVE

Palgrave in the UK is an imprint of Macmillan Publishers Limited,
registered in England, company number 785998, of 4 Crinan Street,
London, N1 9XW.

Palgrave Macmillan in the US is a division of St Martin's Press LLC,
175 Fifth Avenue, New York, NY 10010.

Palgrave is a global imprint of the above companies and is represented
throughout the world.

Palgrave® and Macmillan® are registered trademarks in the United States,
the United Kingdom, Europe and other countries.

ISBN 978–1–137–38519–2

This book is printed on paper suitable for recycling and made from fully
managed and sustained forest sources. Logging, pulping and manufacturing
processes are expected to conform to the environmental regulations of the
country of origin.

A catalogue record for this book is available from the British Library.

A catalog record for this book is available from the Library of Congress.

Typeset by Cambrian Typesetters, Camberley, Surrey, England, UK

Printed in China

Contents

List of Illustrative Material

▶ Insider Perspectives

▶ **Advice from Experience**

▶ **Boxes**

▶ **Tables**

Acknowledgements

I am grateful to the numerous academic staff undertaking PhDs by publication, both in the UK and overseas, who contributed to my focus groups, surveys, emails, phone conversations and interviews. You were the inspiration for this book and gave insight into the range of issues which I have endeavoured to address in the chapters which follow. Thank you for giving me permission to include your thoughts and words.

I am also indebted to various colleagues and the writing group who contributed lively personal stories and provided ongoing support with the content and thinking.

I would also like to extend my thanks to Professor Sally Brown, whose idea it was that this book should be written, whose term 'golden thread' features throughout, and who has been hugely supportive with her advice and contributions. In addition, my thanks go to Professor Ruth Pickford at Leeds Beckett University who has supported my writing and Deb Chapman who has helped with formatting.

I also thank Della Oliver and Helen Caunce of Palgrave for being most encouraging.

I am more than grateful to Rachel and Nick for stoically putting up with the writing process and their great encouragement. I would also like to thank Rowan for her conscientious administrative support and efficiency.

SUSAN SMITH

List of Contributors

The author would like to thank the following (and many others it has not been possible to list) for their help in sharing their ideas and work, and for responding to my questionnaires:

Professor Sally Brown
Professor Phil Race
Kathryn Brown (Leeds Beckett University)
Professor Carlton Cooke (Leeds Beckett University)
Professor Nick Frost (Leeds Beckett University)
Professor Ruth Pickford (Leeds Beckett University)
Nick Sheppard (Leeds Beckett University)
Professor Christopher Cowton (University of Huddersfield Business School)
Lisa Ward (University of Huddersfield)
Professor Janet Hargreaves (University of Huddersfield)
Christine Rhodes (University of Huddersfield)
Dr Sarah Nixon (Liverpool John Moores University)
Professor Chris Rust (Oxford Brookes University)
Charles Buckley (Bangor University)
Dr Nick J. Watson (York St John University)
Mandy Asghar (York St John University)
Dr Andrew N. Brown (University of Canberra), Executive Manager of the People that Deliver Initiative, Denmark.
Lindsay Brigham (The Open University)
Dr Susanne Morris (University of Queensland)
Dr Coralie McCormack (University of Canberra)
Steph Jameson (Leeds Beckett University)
Simon Thomson (Leeds Beckett University)
Dr David Killick (Leeds Beckett University)
Dr Justine Simpson (Leeds Beckett University)
Dr Pauline Fitzgerald (Leeds Beckett University)
Chris Garbett (Leeds Beckett University)
Steve Jones (Leeds Beckett University)

Introduction

The intended readers of this book are those who are contemplating – or, indeed, already undertaking – the challenging task of doing a PhD by published work. PhD routes by published work can be undertaken prospectively from scratch (often called 'prospective', 'planned' or '*ab initio*' routes), or can be completed retrospectively where existing publications relating to a coherent body of work are collated. Whichever route you choose, this book is here to help you. The book aims to give a sense of the reality and challenges of doing a PhD by these routes and is informed by surveys of academic staff in universities in the UK, New Zealand, South Africa and Europe; focus groups; one-to-one interviews and individual telephone calls. It has been designed as an evidence-based handbook threaded with real stories and experiences to enhance the authenticity of the text.

Hofstadter (1979) uses the term 'going meta' for the rhetorical trick of taking debate or analysis to another level of abstraction. This book is a bit of a 'meta' book – I am writing about writing, researching how to write up research and attempting to structure sections on structure. But it has been written to guide you and so, with this in mind, the text addresses 'you'. It is not aimed to be an abstract, distant academic tome but, rather, a guide informed by best practice, grounded in pragmatism and laced with a shot of encouragement. For this reason, questions are posed throughout to facilitate your consideration of your progress and actions.

For some candidates of the PhD by published work route, the process is relatively simple – first, choose the best papers you have written around a coherent theme that are published in peer-reviewed journals. Second, show how you have contributed to the knowledge of your field, identify why your work is original in your field. Third, demonstrate your overall knowledge of your life's work in your viva. For others it is much more challenging. Some may just be starting to write for publication and have a sense that, in a few years, they would like to collate their work into an academic award.

Others may be accomplished academic writers and feel that they may almost have 'enough' journal papers or work in the public domain to enrol for an existing published work award and they then write their synthesis.

Others, after a long career, know they have almost *too wide* a portfolio of work but need help identifying a theme and writing a synthesis. Indeed, for many, structuring the synthesis may be more of a challenge than the research itself (Carter, 2009).Others may be already happy doing their prospective route but need some hints on publishing, writing up their synthesis at the end of their publishing journey or preparing for the viva.

Whether you are feeling daunted dipping your toe in the PhD by published work water for the first time, drowning in it or safely heaving yourself up on the riverbank when you are nearly there, I hope you will find this book helpful at any stage.

In addition, the book contains various features: Advice from Experience, Insider Perspectives, and some activities focused mainly on the practicalities of your synthesis writing. The collated Advice from Experience boxes have been generated from the individual contributions of the researchers, staff and PhD students I surveyed and interviewed. Whether these are viewed just as tips, then that is up to the reader. I think 'tips' devalues the deep reflective academic study involved in PhD work at the highest level and can make the associated advice seems somewhat patronising. One of my respondents mentioned that the candidate uses 'determination, resilience, reflection, courage and persistence' and, if you have all that, then you do not need 'tips'. I now use the word only occasionally specifically to reflect the practicality of advice given from the contributors' real individual experiences of undertaking published work PhDs. Its use is not intended to devalue the award but, rather, to heighten the practical nature of the information, and should be considered in parallel with the more considered and detailed analysis of the individual Insider Perspectives in each of the chapters.

The 31 Insider Perspectives are designed to help bring the book to life and to attempt to dilute the sense that PhDs by publication are dominated by regulatory issues. Hearing others' views also reassured me that I was not alone in drowning in the publications swamp and I hope you find a story with which you can identify. I have given the contributors alternative names but have categorized them to help you relate to them – your story may be similar to their stories. The activities have been tried out on students working towards a PhD by published work and have been refined in light of their comments. There are real-life finished examples of activities and blank templates for you to use either on your own, or as a teaching tool in your writing groups. The completed examples will give you a starting point from which to generate your own material (or even generate your own new frameworks). There are also some tables and boxes which offer collated comparisons. Regulations and requirements vary and change so rapidly and are so specific to your own university that I have used this device sparingly for fear that the moment I published them and linked them directly to a university department, they would almost immediately be out-of-date.

Core to all published work routes, whether retrospective or prospective, is the writing of a synthesis. This encapsulates the content of the papers, points towards new work and outlines the candidate's originality and contribution to knowledge. However, I discovered that the 'synthesis' can be known by a range of terms (an 'exegesis', 'cover story', a 'supporting statement', a 'reflective piece' or even the rather grand 'analytic commentary'). For consistency and brevity, I have referred to it in this book as 'the synthesis'.

Likewise, candidates undertaking a retrospective published work route will not need a supervisor in the traditional sense – their research has been quality assured by the very act of surviving the rigor of the peer-reviewed publication process. Such candidates will be *advised* as to the content of their paper portfolio and the content of their synthesis. However, as most universities still typically allocate *supervisors* rather than advisors (as they are still doing the research and writing the papers, prospective candidates have active supervisors), I have used 'supervisor' as the term of reference in this book for the individual who is the academic advisor. You will see in Chapter 4, that their roles and nomenclature is discussed in some depth.

▶ **The structure of the book**

The book comprises six chapters exploring in an intuitive chronological order, the context of the awards, the practical elements of the award process, how to write effectively for publication and for your synthesis, how to make the most from your supervisor and how best to prepare for your viva.

Chapter 1 considers the different PhD routes in more detail. The specific advantages and challenges of published work routes are explained. If you are still undecided about whether a published work route is the route for you, then the outline of the expectations of retrospective published work routes compared with traditional PhD routes and professional doctorates may help you choose the most suitable way forward. This chapter also explores the expanding portfolio of doctoral programmes in the wider context of global changes in higher education and research. Quality assurance issues relating to the parity of published work routes are also addressed.

Chapter 2 aims to help you understand some of the practicalities of pursuing a published work route and gives you an idea of what it 'looks like'. It includes practical sections on whether you have sufficient publications, why the synthesis has so many alternative titles, and what process and support you might expect from your university if you proceed with a published work route. The whole chapter is peppered with Insider Perspectives and activities to help inform and guide you.

In order to achieve a PhD by published work (whether retrospectively or from scratch) the key thing you need to do is ... publish. Chapter 3, a core chapter, outlines the challenges of initiating and completing the process and has a very practical focus. It addresses improving your success rate in writing for journal article publication; what counts as a publication; and how exhibitions, different forms of media, artefacts and teaching resources could contribute to the total of your submitted works. The chapter also addresses how using peers, networks, communities of practice and journal clubs can enhance your confidence, speed up your submissions and, hopefully, influence your success rate. Wenger's (1998) work on communities of practice can be applied to generating PhD writing support groups and this is considered here.

Chapter 3 also addresses the thorny issue of choosing the best journals specifically for the purpose of gaining a PhD by published work. This includes consideration of the dilemma of whether to aim for top journals or to settle for middle-ranking or newer journals. Top journals are more competitive and may slow down your acceptance rates, which may be problematic on a prospective route. Middle-ranking or newer journals will potentially enable you to publish the required number of articles in a shorter time. Generalist and specialist journal choices are also considered, together with the practicalities of dealing with co-authors and how to attribute work contribution effectively and fairly.

The chapter concludes with a short piece on the value of writing a capstone paper that helps to demonstrate the coherence of your case and how the very act of writing the capstone article and finishing your papers and synthesis can generate ideas for future spin-off publications in new directions.

Chapter 4 deals with the synthesis – the key theoretical piece which illuminates the originality of your thinking, showcases and demonstrates your 'golden thread' of connectivity, and demonstrates how your work has made a contribution to the overall body of work at each stage in its development. For the purpose of this chapter, this coherent theme is referred to as the 'golden thread' – the nub of the thinking that weaves through your work and which you must make sure you elucidate in your synthesis – a fantastic term coined by Professor Sally Brown.

To a certain extent, making a good job of the synthesis prepares you for the viva. It is pretty much guaranteed that you will be asked about the originality of your work, its coherence, how you came up with your 'golden thread' and your contribution to knowledge. Examiners will be assessing whether you show deep reflection in each of these areas. This chapter outlines ways to think reflectively to strengthen your synthesis content and presentation, and this will support the preparation you will need to do for your viva. The core of the chapter focuses on how to strengthen the synthesis to elucidate the core triple whammy from the PhD standard perspective – *originality, contribution to knowledge* and *coherence*. There is a discussion about the different approaches to demonstrate the impact of your work, and some practical frameworks and ideas on how to finish and strengthen your synthesis when most of the content is written.

The chapter is threaded with practical advice and the collated ideas from the surveys, literature, focus groups and individual experiences. The chapter includes examples of how individual candidates generated themes at the beginning of a prospective route and how, for other candidates, collating their retrospective work crystallized proposed themes for their synthesis.

Chapter 5 focuses on working with your advisor and spends some time explaining why, for a retrospective PhD by published work route, your 'supervisor' is really an advisor. The emotions of the whole process are dealt with in some depth, exploring how, if you 'lose' your key advisor/supervisor, then ultimately it may not necessarily feel like a negative experience. Examples of advisors' and supervisors' experiences are included. Real-life tips relating to how to make the most of your advisor/supervisor are included at the end of the chapter.

There are innumerable books focusing on the conventional PhD route viva voce examinations and how to perform well in them. Chapter 6 will focus less on the well-known general advice for viva voce examinations; instead, it concentrates on the specific purpose and structure of the viva for PhD by published work routes.

The worst thing to do in preparation for your viva voce examination is just hope it will 'be all right on the night'. As Race (2007) writes, 'You may *deserve* for it to go well but it is important to take some steps to maximise the likelihood that nothing will go wrong.' It will include how the viva voce examination (or defence) for this route is both similar to and different from the viva for the traditional route, and then concentrate advice around how to prepare to demonstrate to the examiners the originality of your work, your contribution and your work's impact. Discussion about training support, the value of a mock viva voce examination, sample questions and what to expect on the day will help clarify your expectations and help you prepare. The issues of examiners' recommendations and the reality of your future work are also addressed.

1 What is a PhD by Published Work and Why do it?

The introduction in the 1960s of the published work route to a British PhD was a major, if somewhat controversial, innovation (Wilson, 2002), since which time this concept of having a PhD submission based wholly or largely on publications has continued to thrive and expand (UKCGE, 2004). This distinctive route allows the submission of a doctoral synthesis based exclusively or largely on a range of published work and is in contrast to the conventional route to a doctorate, in which candidates who have followed an approved programme of supervised research submit a thesis for examination.

This chapter addresses why you might want to study for a PhD by published work. It will help you decide why you might choose a PhD by published work route over the alternatives and what it may involve in practice. It will also address the changing culture in higher education in the UK and internationally, which has influenced the increasing numbers of university staff enrolling for PhDs in general and, specifically, the PhD by published work. The chapter provides an overview of all the routes, with a focus on outlining the details of the regulations and requirements of the PhD by published work routes (mainly by existing published work and the prospective, gradual route), illuminating inconsistencies and similarities between and within awards. The rationale and suitability for taking this route is explored.

▶ Doctoral awards

The expanding portfolio
A central tenet of all doctoral research is that the work achieved should impact on knowledge in the field, that the candidate should be able to present the work and its impact clearly, and defend it robustly against peer critique. As the UKCGE (2004) report on the PhD by published work awards

states, 'going public is a necessary part of doctoral study and assessment', going on to state that 'most universities would expect the PhDs that they award contain material that is of publishable quality. Publication is then one of the criteria by which these PhDs are judged.'

The concept of publishing doctoral dissertations was adopted in the USA in the early twentieth century and, subsequently, in mainland Europe and the UK. The expense of printing the whole thesis in the early days eventually became the limiting factor in the award of the degree and the practice of making the award on the basis of published journal articles, book chapters or whole books emerged. Hence, the development of the published work degree was, to some extent, actually driven by cost (UKCGE, 1996).

There is a huge range of doctoral programmes. Most universities have a conventional thesis-based route and an expanding portfolio of professional doctorates; however, not so many offer a published work route. A 1996 survey conducted by Wilson (UKGCE, 1996) revealed that of the 73 higher education institutions in England, Wales and Northern Ireland replying to the survey, half of the institutions participating in the survey did not offer the published work route at that time. In the two-year period prior to the survey, only 72 PhDs had been awarded by this route. This represents a very small proportion of all the PhDs awarded by the institutions in the same period. But, since 1996, the provision and uptake of the published work routes and other PhD routes have increased substantially (Watts, 2012). By the time of the UKGCE report in 2004, this had increased to 80 per cent of the responding institutions.

However, they are not always regarded as accessible and inclusive awards. Many universities only offer the existing published work route and prospective (from scratch) published work routes to their own employed staff. Even if the published work routes were available more widely to external candidates, the information about the awards can be difficult to find. It often requires a detailed trawl through the underworld of the university website labyrinth to find a contact phone number, or more detailed guidance, or to explore whether you are eligible to apply as an external candidate.

Research has shown that the growing diversity of doctoral programmes within a globalized higher education environment contributes to knowledge and enhances innovation (Halse and Malfoy, 2010; Lee, 2011). This diversity in doctoral education is part of wider changes in higher education across the globe that has moved from an elite system with few participants to a mass system, 'massification' (Sankey and St. Hill, 2009), with a much larger proportion of the population being involved (Watts, 2012: 1101) and subsequent expansion in global enrolments of *all* doctoral programmes. In addition,

Green and Powell (2005) note changes in modes of study, with a growth in the number of part-time students, equalization of the gender balance and a significant growth in the numbers of overseas students for all PhD routes. This has all occurred in parallel with the increased autonomy and potential variation among higher education institutions offering doctoral study (Morley *et al.*, 2003) and alongside concerns that doctoral awards should be 'fit for purpose' (Park, 2007).

There is general agreement that the doctoral level is crucially and fundamentally about the creation of original knowledge. (The doctoral level is known in the UK as 'Level 8', to align with the framework for Higher Education Qualifications (FHEQ) (QAA, 2008); in Australia as 'Level 10'; and within the European area's Bologna Agreement as 'third cycle'.) However, beyond that, there are many other possibilities and questions to be asked about the purpose of doctoral programmes. Is the objective of study on a grander scale to develop world class ethical researchers? To protect and extend existing disciplines? To create an intellectual elite for a country? To develop economic strength? Or to maximize life chances, and to develop international sustainability? These questions have all been addressed as part of a wider exploration of the short- and long-term aims of doctoral education and Lee (2013) showed how all these purposes were being served by PhD programme initiatives in Australia, the UK, Estonia, Sweden, Germany, Norway and the USA.

From the perspective of the individual PhD candidate (you!), whether it is by the traditional or published work route, you may not be aware of this grander scheme. You may feel so immersed in your own study and the pressures that it generates, that the wider purpose and context of your PhD programme may have passed you by. You may only be aware that many universities, both in the UK and overseas, are now more frequently making PhD awards the gold standard for their staff. Russell Group and 'red brick' universities in the UK have, for many years, used the possession of a PhD qualification as a threshold selection criterion for new academic posts. There is a reason for this: nowadays, to be effective in their university posts, academic staff need to be able to show that they have original thought, can offer a model for critical thinking and evidence to the students they teach and to the colleagues with whom they work. They need to be able to show they can use current research (their own and that of others) to inform their teaching, new research and daily work. Staff need to be able to show to students, colleagues and the wider academic world that they are at the forefront of their discipline, as well as having a sound professional and practical background. They need to demonstrate that they are academically rigorous, and interested in the research process and the findings and evidence that emerge from this activity. It must be said that a PhD is the award which demonstrates these attributes most effectively.

The traditional research doctorate is just one form of doctoral education alongside a range of other PhD programmes including taught PhDs (incorporating elements of advanced coursework), professional doctorates and the different PhD by published work routes. Of all these routes, PhD by published work routes attract the smallest uptake. Many universities which offered this route still only have a handful of successful completions per year (UKCGE, 2004).

Changes in doctoral level education and developing new skills in research students

Watts (2012) discusses a range of different perceptions about the changes in doctoral level education and its increased diversity. She reflects on Cumming's (2010: 25) view that the contemporary doctoral interface is positioned at 'the points where education, training, research, work and career development intersect' and Miller's (2010) view that these intersections are part of a wider skills acquisition model seen globally in higher education that increasingly has employability as its focus.

An HEFCE (2011) report explores a change in doctoral education and, specifically, how the number of women (increased by 15 per cent between 2007–10), international students, part-time, and older candidates now pursuing doctoral degrees has increased, and how PhD by published work applications are now on the rise. This means that universities are compelled to educate a more diverse group of researchers and need to find solutions to address this.

Preparing the next generation of PhD candidates to function successfully and to contribute to today's world requires going beyond the conceptualization of an apprenticeship model to one focused more on a 'communities of practice' model, including the recognition of peers as learning partners. This requires the coordinated efforts of many levels inside and outside a university. Flores and Nerad (2012) describe how this shift has occurred and is still taking place in numerous doctoral programmes around the world. They demonstrate a shift away from a sole one-to-one top-down master to apprentice (professor to student researcher) learning approach to a structured, more complex doctoral learning process within a series of learning communities that operate at multiple levels inside and outside a university. Networks of fellow doctoral students play particularly important roles in this process by peer supporting and mentoring others in a range of formal and informal networks and institutional structures (Boud and Lee, 2008).

Nerad (2012) describes how this approach brings into doctoral education a form of knowledge production that is becoming more socially accountable and, as a consequence of this approach, an emphasis on translational research has emerged (Feldman, 2008; Woolf, 2008). This means that the research process does not stop with the research findings but, rather, translates them into practical applications that respond to societal or business needs. As a result, doctoral candidates are expected not only to know how to undertake quality research, but also how to be competent writers, speakers and team members who can communicate research goals and results effectively inside and outside the university. These are 'translational skills' (referred to as 'generic' skills, in the UK and Australia) and are not only transferable from academic to non-academic settings, but are also necessary to translate research findings into societal applications. The ramifications of this on research education are that the preparation of doctoral candidates needs to include a wider set of competencies beyond the more familiar traditional 'hard' academic ones (Harman, 2008; Manathunga *et al.*, 2009; Nerad, 2004).

As a result of this shift, doctoral education occurs in multiple environments within a number of learning communities. Doctoral education is structured so that the doctoral students become part of a wider community of practice. This will include not only the core professor/student apprenticeship relationship, but also university departmental professional socialization and learning activities, formal and informal peer learning partnerships with local industry, organizations and governments to inform policy (Government White Paper, 1993) and learning through involvement in national and international conferences and more multi-cultural, international learning communities physically and online.

The overall expansion of PhD by existing published work routes exemplifies this shift in doctoral level education. Typical candidates are university academic staff, who are already committed, active researchers but have the opportunity for enhanced career prospects through the acquisition of a PhD. The individual's reflection on their learning, the experience of refining work for publishing and burgeoning research skills to make an original contribution over many years supports the acquisition of these wider skills, which can contribute to increased confidence, career and personal development.

The increased emphasis on skills development through published work routes mirrors the change in perception of the purpose of the PhD itself. Initially, PhD training was criticized (Government White Paper, 1993) as being far too narrow and as producing thinkers insufficiently capable of communicating and collaborating with peers from different disciplines. However, the PhD award has now been interpreted more usefully (Felton,

2008) as broad, high-level training within a cognate discipline with more attention being paid to the ways in which that discipline impacts on others in both the university and beyond. Generic skills have become – to many – an integral part of the doctoral process for all the awards.

What is the real difference between all these PhD awards?

In some ways, it is inadvisable to generalize about the educational experience of a doctoral candidate. Slade (2011) has argued that we can get hung up on rules and the process relating to PhDs in general. She argues that the doctorate is recognition of attainment – whether traditional in form, an honorary doctorate, a doctorate by publication or one in creative practice – and it is *the quality, not process*, that is important and that we should 'interpret the rules with generosity'. Indeed, that said, the content, structure and engagement with a doctoral programme will vary according to the candidates' subject area, personal circumstances and route chosen. But one thing is clear for all UK doctorates (and international ones) – the requirement for 'the main focus of the candidate's work to be their contribution to knowledge in their field, through original research, or the original application of existing knowledge or understanding' (QAA, 2011b).

But the UK QAA Code of Practice includes the published work route with all the other doctoral awards and, hence, this helps little in the specification, transparency and consistency of different, individual published work awards – this state of affairs has precipitated discussion about quality assurance issues for all PhD routes (Wilson, 2002). To understand the difference, the similarities need to be identified – the key similarities of all the doctoral routes are that:

- their academic status is equivalent;
- all the awards confer the title Dr at the end to a successful candidate; and
- all routes emphasize appropriate research methodology and the requirement that the candidate should make a contribution to the advancement of the research field.

There are two key *differences*. The traditional PhD is based typically on a supervised programme of research and the submission of a thesis. For our purposes, the PhD by published work, on the other hand, is based on existing research which has led to a number of coherent publications, each of which has been subjected to peer review. The other key difference is that, with a traditional PhD, the appointed supervisor(s) train the candidate in research methodology and ensure the candidate develops appropriate personal and interpersonal skills. In contrast, with the existing published work routes such training is recognized and evaluated in retrospect on the reviewing of the publications themselves. Some have found this interpretation to be analogous to the acceptability of accredited prior learning (APL) in taught undergraduate and postgraduate programmes (UKCGE, 2004).

However, it is clear that the different awards and programmes offer widely differing *experiences* from different students' perspectives. Hughes and Tight (2013) explored the 'multi-faceted and complex experiences' of students undertaking a range of PhD routes, while exploring the wider questions of modern universities needing to meet the needs of many markets and offering a wide range of routes. The expansion of routes might create some confusion for applicants.

Notable features of the UKCGE (1996) survey were the lack of an obvious pattern in the manner in which institutions offered the route to the published work doctoral degree and some supervisors being insufficiently well-equipped to support new routes. In other ways, this wider range of programmes could be regarded as an improvement. It offers PhD routes to those who may not typically be able to access the traditional route – for example mid-career academic staff, those with clinical and professional backgrounds, or those who have published widely but who have never secured finance to support their studies. Overall, more ready access can only be a good thing.

▶ The wider context

Newer universities, which historically have had a strong professional and technical subject base, are now starting to require new staff to hold PhD qualifications and, increasingly, a PhD is required as an essential selection criterion for the appointment of academic staff to posts. PhDs are also becoming a requirement for existing internal academic staff (who may have been employed for many years before it became a requirement) as a prerequisite for promotion internally, or to move to a different job in another university or overseas.

The PhD by published work award accommodates those whose academic work is of the highest reputation but who may not have had the chance to complete a formal doctorate. In addition, other staff (those who may not have a purely academic post) are increasingly recognizing the need for effective writing, knowledge and critical thinking, and are also undertaking PhDs by a range of routes. There is now a situation where it is not merely the individuals in academic roles who are undertaking PhDs, but also managers, technical staff and learning support staff who are seeking new opportunities for personal and career development, developing skills in research and critical thinking, and enjoying the challenge of improving their scholarly writing, advanced thinking and problem-solving skills.

Doctoral research, is 'knowledge work' (Green, 2009) and 'the traditional PhD is no longer the sole object of concern or the singular sign of value' (p. 240). Lee (2010: 13) has also addressed how the routes to doctoral qualification are 'metamorphosing rapidly' and Nyquist (2002) discusses that, while reconsidering the different routes to achieving a PhD is not something new, 'this time round, the reconsideration of the purposes and future of the PhD degree seems to differ significantly from past assessments'. In parallel, it also seems that the traditional PhD routes are changing in their expectations. Candidates in Scandinavia are required, for all or part of the materials presented for doctoral examination, to have previously been published (Taylor and Beasley, 2005) and, in Australia, while publication of findings on the traditional route is not mandatory, doctoral students and their supervisors are having to deal with new pressures (particularly in arts and social sciences) to produce a range of peer-reviewed publications by the time the thesis is completed (Lee and Kamler, 2008).

What's changing in higher education and what are the new expectations?

Both in the UK and overseas, many universities are now making PhD awards the gold standard for their staff and making the possession of a PhD qualification an essential threshold selection criterion for new academic posts. However, in recent years (since about 2000), growing numbers of universities across the world have been offering postgraduate students a less conventional way of earning a PhD – a doctorate granted on the basis of published work. The traditional PhD route typically involves an individual enrolling as a postgraduate research student for three to five years (longer, if part-time) to undertake a research study linked to an existing body of work in a research department, writing and submitting a thesis in a specific subject area, successfully defending their work in a viva, and then typically being awarded a PhD for their innovative and critical work.

All PhD programmes are tailored and adapted to make sure they prepare future graduates for a range of careers (not purely in research roles, but in industry and business). For example, Manathunga *et al.* (2009) carried out work reviewing PhD students' perceptions of the graduate attributes they developed prior and during their PhD studies, showing the importance of particular skills which were important in their future careers. They discuss how listening to the employment and course experiences of the PhD graduates is an important way of making sure programmes are adapted to prepare future graduates for a range of careers. The traditional route still remains most popular but, in addition, there are now doctoral routes for candidates to find novel approaches to integrating professional and academic knowledge (professional doctorates) and also the route on which this book specifically concentrates, which allows staff that may already be publishing in their own area of interest in a coherent subject area in peer-reviewed journals to use this work for an award (a PhD by published work/PhD by publication).

▶ Different types of doctoral awards

Choosing the right route for you

It is really important you choose the right PhD route. Why? Undertaking any PhD is a commitment and you need to use your time effectively, capitalize on existing work, and think about your career path and your current and future life plans. The following section might help you crystallize whether the PhD by published work route suits you by comparing it with some of the other route options available.

As a result of this change of expectations *for* and *by* university staff, and the changing nature of higher education, different routes to obtain a PhD have opened up. The MPhil/DPhil routes, the more traditionally based substantial thesis routes (typically, 80,000 to 100,000 words), or a taught professional doctorate are suitable for some concentrating on building professional practice. Published work routes and PhDs by portfolio (particularly useful if your subject area is in music or design) widen the pool of available opportunities still further. Some universities provide taught programmes with or without associated published research outputs in the public domain but this depends on the specific regulations of each institution. European doctorates (PhD) may be awarded to candidates undertaking research in the traditional way but whose work is examined by at least two experienced examiners from universities within the European Union. In addition, some universities offer an MPhil by published work (similarly an MA or MSc by research), which are worth investigating. However, MPhils are commonly offered as part of the traditional PhD route and UKCGE (2004) questions the equivalency of offering an award as part of one route and not another.

Traditional route

The traditional PhD route remains popular and has the highest uptake (see Insider Perspective 1.1). Typically, the conventional PhD route involves an individual enrolling as a postgraduate research student to undertake a research study linked to an existing body of work in a research department, writing and submitting a thesis in a specific subject area, successfully defending their work in a viva and then, typically, three to five years later being awarded a PhD for their innovative and critical work. A traditional route PhD is a research-based doctoral programme which usually involves little or no taught element and is often purely academic in nature.

The professional doctorate route

There has been a 30 per cent increase in professional doctoral programmes, since 2005 (Brown and Cooke, 2010). However, there is no substantial research into this growth, whether the awards on offer are 'fit for purpose' or 'good value' for the institution or prospective student, or whether they add a competitive edge to the UK's postgraduate portfolio. A report by Universities UK (2009) stated that, while the professional doctorate sits under the QAA's qualification framework, there still continues to be a difficulty (as with the published work routes) in offering clarity on a specific definition and identification of the nature of the award which would sit consistently across UK institutions.

The aim of professional doctoral programmes is to produce a qualification which, while being equivalent in status, is more appropriate for those pursuing professional rather than academic careers. These are typically rooted in specific practice contexts such as those of education, social work and business, and students are attracted to this route because they wish to extend their knowledge, improve practice and engage in advanced learning in their professional field (Watts, 2009).

Professional doctorates can (as with the traditional thesis-based routes) take between three to four years of full-time study and may be twice as long if studying part-time. Common to all routes is completion of original research, presented as a thesis and (as with a traditional PhD) examined by at least two experts in the chosen field. Usually, a professional doctoral research thesis would relate to real-life issues concerned with professional practice. In many cases, for professional and practice-based doctorates, the candidate's research project will be undertaken in the workplace and so, therefore, have a direct effect on that specific organization's policy and change, as well as improve the individual's practice. The expectation is that the candidate makes a contribution to both theory and practice in their field, and impact on professional practice by making a contribution to professional knowledge. (See Insider Perspective 1.2.)

As indicated, many professional doctorates will also offer a series of modules with a large taught or study-directed element which is formally assessed. These modules typically include the teaching of research methods and critical thinking skills in professional practice. These practice-based PhDs can involve a wide range of outputs varying from product reports, portfolios, artefact dissertations and experimental innovation. The regulations for these awards legitimately allow this, but it has led some to argue that practice-based doctorates have been undertaken on the margins of the academy (Evans, 2010: 67) and for the award status issues to be questioned. Students on these professional doctoral programmes cut across established practices in doctoral education because of the double focus on occupational practice and research. Purists would argue PhDs should be single, focused on research skills and outputs only. Watts (2012) describes how the professional doctoral position is not one of 'clear cut doctoral jurisdiction due to the necessary cross boundary interaction between their workplace, the university and professional practice communities'.

But, putting concerns about the scholarly nature of practice-based doctoral outputs to one side and the 'somewhat slippery' (Seddon, 2010: 220) criteria that govern the standards for the award of 'Doctor', it is this route that has emerged as the main alternative to undertaking a traditional thesis-based PhD route. It clearly suits those graduates who have a professional, rather than a pure scholarly, focus and who are intending to pursue non-academic careers but need to be at the top of their game in research practice as applied to their professional area (Watts, 2012).

PhD by published work route: the basics

You may already have decided that neither professional doctorates nor the traditional routes outlined so far are suited to you. If you have skipped the whole section above because you just know those routes are not for you and you bought this book because you are clear you want to undertake a published work route, then the nitty gritty of the published work routes will be explained now. Indeed, if you do not want to have to undertake taught modules, or be linked to a professional practice area, and you have a port-folio of good publications already, there would be absolutely no reason or sense in doing a professional doctorate. You have presumably bought this book because you are already doing a published work route or are inter-ested in doing it in the future. Indeed, you may already be part way through undertaking a published work route and pondering whether you have enough publications to submit and want to start writing up your synthesis. If this is the case, this book might help you plan for your viva, help improve and focus your synthesis, or help you to work more effectively with your supervisor.

The UK Council for Graduate Education (UKCGE, 1996) has said that publications routes were sometimes 'shrouded in mystery' but, since then, more work has been done to clarify the number of routes available and indi-cate issues for its successful delivery (UKGCE, 2004).That said, the number of institutions offering published work routes is expanding in the UK (UKCGE, 2004). While caution needs to be used in interpreting these figures, there are clear trends showing the published work route is becoming more common across the UK sector. The report was also clear in stating that there is no movement indicating that universities already offering the award in 1996 had withdrawn it subsequently. One could therefore assume from this that the awards offered were viable, had sufficient applicants and could be supported by the offering university.

Basically, there are two key ways of undertaking a published work route: retrospectively and prospectively (from scratch). The most common is the retrospective route. If a university offers a published work route, it will usually be through this route, although they may vary in their nomenclature and requirements; for example, the PhD *with* publication in the theology discipline at the University of Gloucester and PhD by publication and practice at Manchester Metropolitan University. However, let us think first about the PhD by published work routes in general – whether the 'by existing published work', or the less common 'prospective (or *ab initio*/from scratch) route'.

The Quality Assurance Agency, the key regulatory body in the UK states that the:

> PhD by Publication shares many characteristics of a PhD/D Phil via the traditional route and is awarded on the basis of a series of peer-reviewed academic papers, books, citations or other materials that have been published, accepted for publication, exhibited or performed, usually accompanied by a substantial commentary linking the published work and outlining its coherence and significance together with an oral examination. (QAA, 2011(a): 17)

The PhD by published work offers a useful alternative route to gaining a doctorate. Combining the drive for enhanced numbers of completions of doctoral study and the contemporary higher education environment in which given publications are an important measure of an institution's status, research reputation and impact, it seems that publications that are either sole or co-authored within the institution are likely to be encouraged more and more. Most universities across the world offering published work routes typically require the production of a significant body of publications (normally six to 12 single authored articles in refereed journals or the equivalent), together with a synoptic commentary (synthesis) demonstrating how the works together comprise a coherent whole, equivalent to the thesis produced in conventional PhDs and similarly providing evidence of a substantial contribution to the advancement of knowledge. Many universities only accept internal staff or alumni. Other universities do accept external applicants but very often only accept external postgraduates if they are alumni of the university or are at least seven years post-graduation.

There are often criteria attached to the selection of internal staff on the route, too. For example, most regulations state that the published work candidate needs to have been employed at the university for at least one year. Obviously, the answer is to check the regulations carefully for your preferred university. The retrospective route by existing works (often called PhD by existing published work) suits individuals who are already widely published, established researchers, are mid-career, and may have written extensively over many years. Very often, these people have not been in a position to enrol for a conventional PhD and certainly do not want to undertake a PhD from scratch when they already have a suitable body of published work in a coherent area. In my surveys of the PhD by published work candidates, it appeared that all who have successfully completed and enjoyed the published work route have a love of writing, wish to keep on publishing, wish to be part of their university's submitted institutional research assessment exercise work and then arrive at a point where they can, with the addition of a synthesis and a viva, achieve the submission requirements and standard for this academic award. Similarly, the published work prospective route where candidates write up to approximately eight new papers or produce new artefacts/outputs from scratch over a set period of time suits those staff who may already have an established research subject area and wish to convert key findings into a set number of sole or co-authored publications/outputs.

Both these published works routes suit those researchers who have published/or who will have published at least as much as would be required for a conventional PhD. Indeed, Lee (2010), in her discussion of different routes to doctoral qualification in what she refers to as 'contested space', states that a PhD by published work is not a single monograph or huge dissertation but, rather, 'a series of shorter pieces, which are assessed by a range of different readers and reviewers before they are submitted for a final examination' (p. 13) and this may suit those who like to write and acquire outputs singly or collaboratively over a longer period of time.

'A rose by any other name': the synthesis

The final examination for the published work routes involves the addition of the synthesis and the final viva. As you will have noted, the synthesis is known by a range of names and you may recognize it in your university regulations as something else: possibly 'a portfolio summary', 'a cover story', 'an exegesis', 'an analytical commentary', 'a reflective summary', 'an overview' or 'a narrative account'. Whatever the summarizing piece is called in your regulations, the inclusion of it is critical to a PhD by published work award. It requires the candidate to summarize, reflect on and synthesize all the submitted independent papers, chapters and artefacts into a whole written piece that supports and relates to the 'coherent thread' of the work. As part of this and as a critical review of the collated publications, the synthesis needs to make a distinct contribution to the knowledge or under-standing of the subject and show evidence of originality. This is the intellec-tual challenge and the real nub of this route's doctoral work. Practical advice on the writing of the synthesis for PhD by published work candidates is addressed in Chapter 3. While 'published work' can be in a variety of forms – artefacts, resources, films – the university requirements for the synthesis request a standard written form.

Unsurprisingly, the synthesis lengths vary hugely depending on university requirements. Both my own survey and the UKCGE (2004) survey showed word limit ranges between 3,000 and 25,000 words.

▶ The international situation

Published work PhD routes are becoming increasingly common worldwide. They are well-established in The Netherlands, Canada, New Zealand, Scandinavia and Australia. However, PhD by published work routes and the traditional routes can sometimes be rather blurred and overlap. For example, very often candidates doing the traditional PhD route in China and in many northern European countries (e.g., Sweden, Finland and Estonia) have a requirement that they, as doctoral candidates, have to publish three articles in peer-reviewed journals *before* being allowed to proceed to the viva stage (Powell and Green, 2007). This is somewhat different from the UK's assessment requirement for traditional PhDs, which is for subject specialists to conduct an oral examination in private without any prerequisite of publication. Lee (2013) states that the main knock-on-effect from this is that doctoral students doing the traditional route can take a much longer time to graduate.

In Sweden, Australia and Canada, doing a PhD by published work in some disciplines is actually a relatively common way of getting a PhD. The science model of apprenticeship of young (non-staff) students with supervisors and joint publications has been operating for some time – it is not considered as a prospective route, but a PhD is often awarded retrospectively after many years when 'sufficiency' is reached. In Germany, however, there is a slightly different model. Their PhD by existing published work route is for university staff – but typically most of these staff often work on temporary contracts on a range of funded research projects. These projects are run in collaboration with industry over many years of their career and can be an iterative process. The candidate ultimately submits a portfolio of published work to the university's specific thesis committee. The university committee panel will assess the work and frequently ask the student to add to it on several occasions to meet the required sufficiency. Only at the point where the sufficiency of the research is approved will the student write a synthesis. Sometimes, German universities do not require this synthesis element at all (or a final viva examination); the whole body of research work on its own being regarded as enough to meet the standard. Very often the lecturer cannot become a full-time, permanent member of staff at the university without their PhD (often worked for over the duration of many years). That said, the German 'excellence initiative' has invested heavily in doctoral education and research for graduate schools to train PhD students, support centres of research excellence and nine elite universities. As a result, top class researchers are now choosing to stay in Germany, appreciating its vibrant and well-invested research culture (Mechan-Schmidt, 2012).

As stated, PhDs by published work routes are common in most Scandinavian countries, Belgium and Australia (UKCGE, 1998), and there has been an appetite to support these awards. Many parts of Europe have adopted regulatory structures that are typified by their flexibility in terms of the way the candidate's programme of study is carried out, and the nature and content of the doctoral submission. This contrasts with the situation in many UK institutions, where two models of PhD exist separately – one based on the traditional individual programme of research training leading to the oral defence of a doctoral thesis and the other based on published works.

However, in other parts of the world (South Africa, for example) the PhD by published work route has been 'viewed with scepticism ... and its uptake has been limited' (Grant, 2011: 245). In these universities, the academic staff mainly undertake the conventional route to a PhD and then move into traditional research-focused academic careers.

▶ How has the experience of undertaking a PhD by published work changed?

Beyond Europe, Australia and Canada, the notion of PhD by publication is still 'sometimes seen to be problematic – counter-intuitive, even' (Lee 2010: 26).

For example, in South Africa and the Far East, a PhD by published work is a relatively new phenomenon (Grant, 2011: 248) and has had its problems for students starting out on a brand new route. Grant explores the issues of embarking on a PhD by publication in a university in South Africa, where 'the rules for publication-based study have only recently been accepted at the level of the University Senate'. It can be very tough for new candidates, who may be the first to embark on this route in their country or institution. There may be few supervisors skilled in this route from which to choose, no detailed guidelines, no academic network of those who have successfully completed their study, and no comparable theses in institutional libraries to study and compare structural and style preferences. In her work about the transformation of doctoral studies, Grant describes how, in early 2008, the only 'official' guidance available for her published work route were in the 'General academic rules and the rules for students' which only briefly outlined the format required.

However, things are improving and, as the number of candidates has increased and universities are now regularly provide this route, the guidance provided is generally becoming more detailed and clear. However, university requirements across the world differ – specifically, around the number and type of core outputs required and the vague guidance on sole and joint authorship. In Norway, typically, only four papers are required in international peer-reviewed journals compared with, say, eight in the UK; this raises questions about the parity of the awards. Very often, Norwegian academics have to write in English, which is more difficult than writing in the mother tongue.

The crux of all these variations and unclear guidelines is that, if you choose the published work route, you must take responsibility as the candidate to seek advice and clarification about the submission requirements from the university you choose, and make sure the supporting infrastructure suits you, your work style and your career timeline. University regulations often provide little clarity on the number of articles required for a doctorate by publication; neither do they offer guidance as to the purpose, format or length of the accompanying documentation. Draper (2012) has argued this could leave candidates feeling vulnerable or cynical. But perhaps this diversity of models is the crux of PhD by published work routes. Draper (2012) has also argued that we need to have evidence that the PhD by publication is similar in length, scope and quality to a conventional doctorate, yet warns against too precious a view of the quality of modern doctorates. As he says, 'More than in any other area in universities, PhDs by research should surely be about recognising attainment: about judging the outcome and product, regardless of the means and process by which it was arrived at.'

The really tricky questions arise in disciplines in which academic peer-reviewed journals are not the benchmark of published quality, such as in journalism or creative writing. While it may be awkward to make such comparisons, an in-depth piece of reflective investigative journalism for a respected newspaper or well-regarded magazine is surely as significant a contribution to knowledge as material submitted for more traditional doctorates? Equally, an award-winning novel or script may involve creative and evaluative skills appropriate for recognition within a higher education institution. Doctorates in creative fields bring other standardization and consistency issues. As Slade (2011) discusses, what forms of composition, what artwork, what designs should count as contributions to knowledge at the highest level, and who is the best person to adjudicate this and make such a judgement?

In addition, Draper (2012) has identified a huge range of word counts for the synthesis/reflective work component for published work awards across the sector in Britain alone. Lee (2010: 12–13) discusses the wide range of requirements for the synthesis and its portfolio presentation in Sweden, and Niven and Grant (2012) the varied regulations and requirements in South Africa. While Slade (2011) questions the variability over the 'correct' length, she also asks whether, ultimately, all this diversity is actually particularly beneficial, arguing that its very variability shows educational flexibility and awards that are designed to be fit for purpose.

Quality assurance and parity issues

There is much overlapping and blurring between the process and outputs of all the different PhD awards, and it is questionable why the distinctions by all these numerous titles are needed at all. In fact, Clarke and Powell (2009) have argued that the higher education sector in the UK is in danger of prolif- erating the kinds of nomenclature available for this level of doctoral study without addressing the real purpose of the distinctions.

In the main, published work routes (and other atypical doctoral routes) must be considered within the same quality domain as traditional doctorates and this has been achieved, on the whole, in practice. However, Clarke and Powell (2009) have indicated that issues of quality differ across the various forms of doctoral study – particularly in PhDs by published work, doctorates in the creative arts and 'taught' doctorates. In particular, they address the need to take care in the initial assessment of the ability of the candidate to be able to produce independent research. While it may be the case that a candi- date's publications do not provide direct evidence of successful training in research methods, there is typically an acceptance in institutional regula- tions where such awards are on offer that success in the process of publica- tion itself provides evidence of the ability to carry out research through to completion. Care is obviously required when assessing whether that ability is of an independent kind – that is, the levels of collaboration and the kinds of input made by various individuals named as collaborative joint authors need to be checked to ensure that the successful candidate can continue as an independent researcher in a sustained and creative way.

The UKGCE (2004) report addressed quality control of PhD by publication routes and summarized key issues in an earlier report (UKGCE, 1996), which institutions have been encouraged (with some success) to consider and address. For example, the eligibility criteria, the time period and location restrictions of publications, synthesis word limits, the roles of advisors/ supervisors, evidence to prove candidates were trained in research method- ologies, variability in sufficiency and the rationale for fee structures. In addi- tion, differences in the composition of the submission through the traditional and published work routes may lead to debate about the appropriateness of the traditional thesis to a candidate's future career as a trained researcher, where the recognized badge of achievement is commonly high-quality, refereed publications. The speed of knowledge change and the practical concerns of national and international research assessment activity mean that priority is attached to publishing; it therefore makes sense that training in research publications would seem to demand recognition as an essential component of traditional PhD training programmes (UKCGE, 2004).

The viva voce examination in both the traditional route and the published work route is also significant as a mark of quality to assess the recognition of contributions from others – that is, by close questioning of the candidate about their *own* ideas and the coherence of the work presented. The UKCGE (2004) report also addresses the issues surrounding some discrepancies across different universities in the UK and overseas about whether external examiners for the viva should be appointed with input from the candidate with regards their suitability for selection.

The solution to all this diversity should probably not be some one-size-fits-all pan-global published works doctorate, an extension of the Bologna process needing extensive monitoring and audit: this would be impulsive and overly bureaucratic. Any solutions to the issue of parity need to begin with discussion in the global scholarly community about equity, parity, and the drawbacks and benefits of diversity.

▶ PhD by existing published work (retrospective route)

What does it look like and whom does it suit?
This retrospective route (also known as the 'existing published work route') tends to suit individuals who are already widely published, are mid-career and may have written extensively over many years (see Insider Perspectives 1.3 and 1.4). Candidates are usually experienced researchers with work of national standing who may have worked on a range of projects and have a portfolio of work in the published domain from which they can select specific papers around a particular theme as the basis of their submission. Unsurprisingly, these individuals are often not keen to enrol for a minimum of *another* five years to undertake a PhD from scratch when they already have a suitable body of work in a coherent area. Most universities only accept postgraduates of at least five years, with a Masters, or at least some evidence that indicates some formal research training. The value of the flexibility of the published work approach is clear, too – this route supports those who have family and personal commitments, and particularly allows those

Insider Perspective 1.3

I am an academic member of staff who had had multiple part and full-time contracts in probably four universities over 14 years. I had had two long periods of maternity leave. However, over 12 years or so I had kept on writing, sometimes intensely and sometimes not very much. I was writing about assessment feedback and actively embedding the findings and the wider evidence into my education practice in the classroom. It was clear I had a theme and it was clear that it would be stupid and a waste of time to start a traditional PhD from scratch when I already had a wodge of publications. I didn't want to waste that work ... Some universities are funny regulations-wise and they only let you submit for a PhD by publication retrospectively if all the work is done (i.e. submitted to the quality journals) while you are employed by that specific university itself. I think this is tough if you have had multiple workplaces. Where I did it though, as long as you were a member of staff you could enrol for this route and use your published works, if they were good enough, to achieve a PhD. It was win–win. I kept on writing and submitting and revising and I only enrolled for a year when I was ready to plan my reflective synthesis, this kept the cost down and I kept on adding publications to my CV – a good route for me.

Janet, reflecting on how she chose her PhD by published work, UK

Insider Perspective 1.4

There were personal drivers to be recognized. I wanted to prove myself as a 'serious' academic writer – an item on a bucket list I think ... I changed, I contributed to the field, I theorized what I was doing and (gradually and tentatively) became a person with an academic voice. I wanted to revisit my published papers, not because I wanted to celebrate them but to tell the story of emergence, to trace a slow and sometime painful trajectory ... Once the proposal was approved by our Higher Degrees Committee, I felt I was halfway to my destination and I became unstoppable.

Louise, within five years of retirement, South Africa (retrospective route)

working part-time to carry on writing up their work for publication. This route can be known by a variety of different names: 'PhD by published work', 'PhD by publication' and 'PhD by existing published work' are all titles I discovered on my trawl through university research award websites from around the world. This last award – PhD by existing published work – is significant; the title emphasizes the notion that it is a retrospective, quality-assured qualification.

Whereas a 'prospective' qualification for a PhD generates a body of super-vised new work from its beginning to its end, usually covering a period of five years, PhD by published work retrospective routes looks at a portfolio of work around a core theme which is part of a wider body of work. Not only do candidates, as part of the first stage of applying for the retrospective published work route, have to provide a list of papers they wish to submit around their core research theme, they also have to submit a full curriculum vitae (CV) detailing all their publications and conference presentations. This can ensure the application panel that the candidate has a track record of researching and writing up, and a clear history of active researching individu-ally or in collaborative research groups.

In addition, at a couple of UK universities, the award PhD *with* publication is available. This involves the submission of peer-reviewed publications but, instead of a synthesis of 10,000 to 12,000 words, candidates write a longer systematic review (often of 25,000 words) of the literature in which their publications are embedded. As part of this, and similar to the synthesis, the individual's original contribution to knowledge has to be evident and criti-cally appraised. The registration period for this award is usually longer, at two years, and the citations in the systematic reviews are extensive (many were up to 1,000 citations). The same criteria for internal and external exam-iners apply as for other routes.

Criticisms and disadvantages of the retrospective/existing PhD by published work route

On reviewing the literature and surveying a range of current candidates undertaking the PhD by existing published work route, there are a range of issues they addressed which illuminated some of the key concerns and diffi-culties with this route. In the sector, both in the UK and abroad, there is still no clear consistency and consensus on its length, purpose or format. There are many differences in university approaches to this award, both in the UK and overseas, which indicates that it is essential to read and to understand the award regulations and requirements, and to seek advice prior to registering.

Some academic staff seem to perceive published work routes in some disciplines to be a less demanding route than the traditional PhD. To me (and, indeed, to the degree awarding bodies), it is clearly equally hard work – work that requires commitment, self-motivation, critical thinking, and simi-larly high standards of writing and research. If colleagues in a particular discipline have perceptions about an award, it can be tiresome and difficult to have constantly to defend one's achievements and value, and this can potentially lead to reduced confidence in the perceived value and status of the award.

In addition, different universities' views on the synthesis/doctoral state-ment (which summarizes the work) are varied, too. A synthesis might have a range of nomenclatures and varying requirements for length, content and inclusion criteria. These inconsistencies may be perceived to contribute to the absence of a sense of parity regarding the award and its robustness.

A further disadvantage with this route is that it may be difficult to find a university to sponsor you. Very often, universities only offer this route to existing internal staff. Critics of this route have seen it as an easy option because of the admission regulations. They have seen it as 'a form of concession to normal academic standards' (Wilson, 2002), citing the fact that, in some universities, eligibility for the route is restricted to internal members of the university staff. The UKCGE (2004) survey confirmed this, showing 18 per cent of universities offered published work routes to their internal current academic staff only, and only 13 per cent opened the routes to all (i.e. restrictions regarding eligibility except appropriate academic qualifications). That having been said, this report generally showed progress on a slow trend to the broadening of eligibility criteria compared with the data submitted in the comparable UKCGE (1996) report. Such severe restrictions on eligibility (despite their having become more inclu-sive in recent years) foster the suspicion that the route is an easy option for a favoured minority, thereby lowering its esteem in the eyes of some of the academic community.

▶ PhD by published work (prospective route)

What does it look like?

As mentioned above, there is another published work route – the prospective route (alternatively known as the '*ab initio*' route), where candidates seek, while adding to their publication record, to produce from scratch a body of work in a coherent subject area and gain their award through an incremen-tal approach. Many universities only accept internal staff candidates who are already active researchers for this planned route and indeed many universi-ties do not offer this option at all, preferring to stick to the existing published work or traditional routes only.

For the prospective award, a programme of research is undertaken the principal focus of is the preparation and compilation of a portfolio of papers produced during the enrolled period of candidature (i.e. not prior to admission, or used as part of the basis for admission). Many universities do accept a backdating of up to two years of peer-reviewed publications but usually stipulate that no more than 50 per cent to 60 per cent of the total publications are backdated. All the papers/outputs need to have been formally accepted for publication by a peer-reviewed journal, in press or in print at the time of examination. Again, peer-reviewed book chapters are sometimes acceptable (depending on the university regulations), provided that they have been formally accepted for publication, or are in press or in print at the time of submission of the thesis. Guidelines for co-authoring are usually similar to that of the PhD by existing published work award. Where one or more of the submitted papers or chapters are co-authored, they should collectively be preceded by a clear statement of the intellectual contribution of the candidate to the submitted papers signed by all of the contributing authors.

Typically, this portfolio of published work must be accompanied by a synthesis which is normally of between 10,000 and 12,000 words (depending on the university's regulations) and which must not include *new* data or results. Results or data presented in the attached papers may be integrated into the synthesis with results and data from literature in order to develop and evaluate the argument presented.

Individuals are likely to take this route as an alternative to registering to undertake a part-time PhD over five or more years. Incrementally achieving publications in this way means there is less risk of failure, which is a recognized problem among academics undertaking traditional routes. Outside commitments, promotions and other interruptions can make it difficult for academics undertaking traditional routes to find the time to study part-time alongside a full-time job. At least by taking this prospective route, if that happens, candidates are still likely to have publications evidenced on their curriculum vitae to show for their endeavours.

Sometimes finding a supervisor for this prospective route can be a challenging process – they have to supervise *and* quality assure your research skills, *as well as* encourage you to write for publication at the same time. The pressures of your writing papers of a sufficiently high standard for peer review (whether individually or collaboratively), as well as honing research and reflective/analytical skills for the ongoing projects which you may be writing up, can represent a substantial workload for any supervisor.

Prospective PhD by published work: the international state of play

The prospective publication route is popular in Scandinavian countries and The Netherlands. Again, there is variability in the regulations for what is regarded as sufficient published work to be in the published domain by the time of the final viva. It is quite common, for example, for researchers to accumulate publications from a registration date with the purpose of constructing a PhD. As discussed, these students on the prospective route in The Netherlands require a somewhat different model of supervision from the more common retrospective model. The supervisor guides the students through the entire five-year publication period (not simply supporting the writing of the synthesis in the final year as for the existing published work route candidate). The supervisor also needs to be able to assist the candidate in planning work to turn into publications, advising on what journals to target. They will also be advising on the research skills and quality assuring the studies, as the students will be publishing *as* they *undertake* the research. This model tends to be attractive to candidates and the universities them-selves, training candidates even more directly as researchers, and boosting the host department's publication record.

In The Netherlands, the range of rules and regulations for this kind of PhD are diverse. Typically, four or five articles in a coherent area have to be written for peer-reviewed journals; for Social Sciences, Medicine and Science, an introduction and a conclusion/discussion chapter (as with a synthesis) have to tie those articles together to form a coherent piece of work. These articles should represent a similar substantial piece of work commensurate with the conventional thesis. The articles can be co-authored (the supervisor is often the co-author) but the supervisor has to verify that the candidate has done most of the work. In the Netherlands, there may not be any fees for this approach; the supervisor's faculty receives a financial lump sum from the research department of the university when the final thesis is accepted and the viva (which is often complex with many regula-tions and fixed procedures) has been successful. At the beginning of the five-year registration period, the supervisor will ask the candidate to write a proposal for all the articles and how they fit together (similar to the proposal for the formal confirmation of registration in the UK); however, this seems to vary quite considerably across the different universities in Europe.

This prospective award is available at universities in Europe and Australia, However, it is often not referred to as an '*ab initio*' or 'prospective route' but, rather, as the standard PhD by published work. The view is that that you will publish a certain number of peer-reviewed papers over a set time period (for example, three years at the University of Canberra in Australia), usually up to a maximum of five years. This route costs three to five years' of fees (as you use the services of the university and your supervi-sor over the whole period), unlike the retrospective PhD of existing published work, where you only pay the supervisor/advisor for the work they do supporting you through the generation of the theme and content of your synthesis (usually, for one year). Many candidates taking this route talked about how they had to define, from a regulatory and volume perspective, what the PhD by published work with their supervisor 'looked like' to persuade a supervisor to take on the role.

Benefits of the prospective route

Academic staff are likely to take this route as an alternative to registering to do a part-time PhD over five or more years, since incrementally achieving publications in this way means there is ultimately less risk of career failure through lack of published work en route. (See Insider Perspective 1.5.)

There are several universities in the UK where this planned publication route is available and many candidates have found it extremely valuable and an excellent opportunity to publish as they 'learn and earn'. However, high priorities are the need for a clear plan and an excellent focus on time management, together with an understanding of the review times for journals. Those who have successfully completed this route indicated that they often had ring-fenced, scholarly activity time integrated into their annual appraisal and performance reviews to ensure they were supported in achieving the PhD. Others comment on the developmental element to this approach, indicating the satisfaction they had in developing their writing skills over time, both individually and in different research teams. Other benefits involve using and learning about the suitability of different research methodologies for different projects, and how the process of writing up each paper catalysed ideas for their future work and next publication.

Insider Perspective 1.5

My institution offered both routes (retrospective and prospective) but only to alumni and current employed staff. I was in a new academic post working in an education research unit. I was working on the beginning of my first publication. But I was working in a unit where publishing was encouraged and I was working in an innovative and coherent area where it was relatively easy to see the links between the ideas I had for the papers I wanted to write and the themes generated from my work. I enrolled and have to write six papers from scratch in five years but I think, because of the nature of the unit and the job and the allocated time to write, I will do this. That is why I chose it – I could do it retrospectively but would have to wait for at least five years to enrol while I do the work. This way I can get it done as part of my job to a clear timescale. This suits me and but I have to be pretty focused.

Nicole, early career researcher with a Masters but no PhD, reflecting on choosing a PhD by published work (prospective route)

Critiques of the prospective PhD by published work route

Writing peer-reviewed publications for the prospective route within the required registration period might potentially compromise the quality of the papers submitted. Colleagues have noted that there could be concerns that the prospective route might subtly change the role of the supervisor, who then might have to help the candidate 'play the publication game' rather than encourage the candidate to think deeply and critically about the content of the ideas in the papers, or as part of the longer research journey which is evident as part of the existing works route. There might be times when a supervisor, however committed, might have to push students to finish and submit papers within the time frame when, actually, they might prefer their candidate to have more time for maturation of the ideas and critical consideration.

Supervisors of students undertaking the planned route have discussed instances when a borderline paper could be submitted to a high quality journal which refused it, only to be accepted by a lower quality journal which might have a less robust peer-review process. Some brand new journals are desperate for papers and, in order to facilitate getting their candidate through in the time, some supervisors with a good knowledge of the new journal market and a network of editors could be tempted to contact the editors of these journals and encourage their students to submit their papers to them … knowing that these journals turn papers around quickly and, as a result, condoning and having a less robust peer-review process. It is a hard balancing act for the supervisors. Supervisors know that, to mitigate this possibility, their candidates should be encouraged to submit to journals which have a high impact and a robust peer-review process. However, rejection from these journals on the grounds that the article is not sufficiently good can delay the student and compromise completion within the publication period.

There is a potential danger with this system that, if students and staff 'play the game', the critical peer-review process – which is the quality assurance mechanism by which the research work is assessed as accurate, methodologically sound and ethical – the prospective route could lead to a dilution in the quality of the submitted research and, hence, the quality of the papers published. By the stage of a candidate's viva, the examiners are then only able to question the coherence, robustness and originality of the submitted synthesis, and are powerless to comment on the quality of the published papers, whatever they may think.

2 Understanding the Practicalities and Process of Doing a PhD by Published Work

This chapter is designed to help raise your awareness of some of the practicalities of undertaking a PhD by published work and explores the pros and cons of studying for a PhD by the published work route. The issues of how much published work is 'sufficient' will be addressed and a 'sufficiency' activity is included with which to assess whether you have enough papers and artefacts for submission. The thorny question of sufficiency (which varies tremendously from institution to institution) will be addressed more holistically to help you decide which pieces of work to submit and what types of work might be acceptable. Authentic examples of individuals' experiences at different stages are dotted throughout the chapter to enhance the realism and offer reader support.

The chapter ends with an outline of the different stages of the award. Some of the key issues to expect during the process will be discussed and illustrated with examples. The availability of the route, the obstacles (Willis, 2010) and the restrictions relating to application will be addressed. This section will also offer advice to candidates on how best to comply with regulations and admission requirements which, as you will discover, are many and varied in their manifestations across the sector.

▶ Pros and cons of the PhD by published work routes

I discussed the advantages and disadvantages of the published work route with colleagues in the course of writing this book. Box 2.1 presents a summary of their thoughts and conclusions.

Box 2.1 The pros and cons of the PhD by published work routes

Pros	Cons
You present and publish as you go, building your academic career and profile – even if you do not submit, you will have good peer-reviewed publications as outputs anyway which can be submitted to your university's Research Excellence Framework (in the UK) or equivalents.	Can feel lonely and isolating and you need to be very organized, self-directed and good at time management.
It feels 'satisfying and rewarding' and offers a route to people who may have been publishing for years in a core area and had never thought of doing a PhD but now their university requires staff to have one.	Sometimes need to be very resilient to cope with repeated major revisions to submitted papers.
You can be part-time and take a career break and still just keep on writing over time. There are opportunities to step on or step off the PhD pathway as other commitments intervene, as long as communication with the supervisor is clear and regulations are adhered to.	Sometimes, it can be difficult to find a supervisor familiar with the published work route for the longer time span of the planned publication route and for synthesis guidance in the existing published work route.
If you have been on a taught traditional route or an Ed D and withdraw, you might be able to write up some of your course outputs for journals as part of a submitted PhD by publication.	Perceived status and prestige – 'some people just don't think it is as good as a traditional route with a thesis and the exclusive admission criteria for the award (i.e. internal university academic staff) has its critics who perceive it as an easy option for the favoured few' (Wilson, 2002).

→

Pros	Cons
The cost of study can be lower for a PhD by existing published work. Students tend to be part-time. The fees cover a much shorter period, as you enrol to write your synthesis/ reflective account usually for a 12-month registration period (UKCGE, 2004).	It can be quite self-exposing at viva time. You present your life work – 'Here I stand with all my work.'
Suits all types of academic staff in different subject specialisms. You may not need to submit papers – if you are in an arts-based field and have creative outputs in the public domain, there may be an opportunity to use these artefacts, too (e.g. exhibits, performance, film, patent records as long as they are in the public domain as a permanent record).	Especially with retrospective routes for PhD by existing published work, if you did not have a plan 10 years ago when you started writing, it might be difficult to find a coherent theme. That is, 'it is tricky to retrospectively shoe-horn diverse papers into a post hoc theme'.
The publications are peer-refereed in your published journals so an examiner would find it difficult to argue that they do not meet the grade.	Published work sufficiency, regulations and the award names vary markedly in different universities across the world. This can be confusing. Not frequently offered and, when they are, are often not open to external applicants.

▶ Sufficiency for the PhD by published work (retrospective route)

Typically, potential applicants for the degree will ask how many publications are needed. While the answer to this question allows the selection of suffi-cient work for the submission, what *really* matters is how these papers have contributed to knowledge in the field and the impact they have made.

Clearly, it is important to exclude any of your publications that weaken the cohesion and dilute the critical message, even if they may be high-quality and deserving in their own right.

So, how much work will you need to form a suitably acceptable body of work that is sufficient for your university? Do you have sufficient now, or are you going to have to wait a little longer before you are in a position to apply for your PhD by published work (retrospective route). The key issue here is that not only do universities change their requirements quite frequently, but also that universities differ in their regulations and expectations for submission. It is therefore vital that you check the guidelines and make sure you stick to them. Planning towards submitting the right amount and type of work is a vital part of the process.

The general view is that most universities offering this route require the production of a 'significant body of publications' (typically, six to 12 articles/outputs in refereed journals or the equivalent), together with a synoptic commentary (the synthesis) demonstrating how, together, the work comprises a coherent whole. The complete submission should be approximately equivalent to the size of a thesis produced by a student undertaking the conventional PhD route and (as with all PhDs) provide evidence of a substantial contribution to the advancement of knowledge.

▶ Insider perspectives: sufficiency

Insider Perspective 2.1 illustrates the ease with which some individuals can select high-quality focused publications from a large, more diffuse portfolio.

Insider Perspective 2.1 Sufficiency

Ten years ago I got my PhD by publication. I had been writing and publishing for years. In the end I used 12 publications in total, of which two were sole-authored book chapters and nine were papers. Of all the publications, eight reported on primary research and the remaining two were based on secondary research, either because their intention was to disseminate the research literature more widely, or because the papers were more theoretical and polemical. I excluded a lot of my long list of publications (I didn't think they were such high quality as the majority of those selected) and actually wrote one more capstone article to lead nicely into the synthesis writing.

Professor, now 10 years post PhD by published work (retrospective route), after 30 years working in higher education, UK

Wilson (2002), in his single-case study of the PhD by published work route at the University of Hertfordshire, described how feedback over time from assessors and examiners moved towards a consensus that paper numbers in excess of 10 publications were positively discouraged. He also gave an example of how some of the more recent successful submissions have been based on as few as three published works.

Universities will only count papers in the published domain which have been peer-reviewed in journals which have an ISBN number. All the published works must be written around an intellectually coherent theme(s) – or, as I like to call it later in this book, the 'golden thread' – which unites the subject matter of the papers/artefacts.

You may have written and produced a huge portfolio of artefacts, book chapters and journal articles over the years and decide to select those which showcase your 'golden thread' most effectively. You are in a lucky position, if you can do this. It is still important to remember that this sub-set must show coherence and be sufficient in its own right. The definition of 'sufficiency' varies with each institution. Some specify that a certain number of single-authored works must be submitted; others do not. Some specify a 'recent' in their submissions list and do not accept publications more than five or 10 years old. Some institutions require candidates to show they have published recently and that their final publication for submission must have been within the last two years before submission (UKCGE, 2004).

You will also have to submit a full curriculum vitae which illustrates and details all your independent and collaborative work and that lists all your publications. This will show the award selection panel that you are a researcher capable of undertaking collaborative or individual research to the equivalent standard of a traditional PhD qualification. It shows them you have written for peer-reviewed journals and this allows them to approve the application at the required standard.

In the majority of universities, core 'published work' only takes the form of journal papers. However, sometimes candidates may wish (and be allowed by their university's regulations) to include monographs and peer-reviewed book chapters. However, the tide now appears to be turning against the inclusion of book chapters in submissions for PhDs by published work. Some universities have now disallowed them, even if they have been through a rigorous peer-review process. Those that do allow them rigorously review the contribution of the author, usually only allowing those that have made a sole substantial contribution to the book. It is therefore of great importance that you check your regulations to see whether book chapters are allowed as part of your portfolio of work. (See Insider Perspective 2.2.)

Insider Perspective 2.2 Sufficiency

This seemed to be the route that suited me despite the fact all my publications were not in a coherent area and, indeed, I thought I didn't have enough publications in one coherent area to be commensurate with a PhD equivalency. Three years before I submitted, I had 15 publications over a 12-year writing period, not all of them were in a coherent subject area and not all in peer-reviewed journals. I had no book chapters at all, had some work that was co-authored and of it most was actually authored solely by me. What I did have was a love of writing and a desire to contribute to my area of academic interest (interprofessional learning and critical reflection). I was advised to review my portfolio of work, identify a coherent intellectual path and focus, and be more discerning with the journals I submitted to.

Susan Smith, mid–career, completed PhD by published work (retrospective route), UK

You should avoid submitting newsletters and conference proceedings, unless there has been a rigorous selection of the content by a panel of editors and your regulations allow them. It is clearly worth being sensible about choosing the papers where your co-authors can confirm your contribution. Sponsored research available only to the sponsors or with restricted access is usually not permitted to be used in doctoral submissions, but this remains a debatable issue, particularly as many 'conventional' theses are placed on restricted access by the awarding universities for reasons of intellectual property rights (Wilson, 2002).

Some universities have a broader definition of 'published work'. Candidates from creative and arts areas may submit 'exhibited art works' and other media as *part of* a wider written portfolio. Work needs to be sufficiently in a 'constant form' and accessible enough to peer review to be considered as disseminated and published. Art works, for example, are published in the sense that they have been exhibited in major galleries and are thus regarded as being in the public domain. It is probably fair to say that, while most universities still want peer-reviewed journal articles as the nub of the submission, many university regulations now allow submission of peer-reviewed teaching materials, artefacts, art from collated exhibitions, films of dance and performance, and other media in the public domain. For example, the Open University, in their regulations for PhD by published work, accept digital media, 3D artefacts 'with written contextualisation' (UKCGE, 2004), film, software and audio files as long as they are provided in a suitable format for viewing (and are in the public domain) and can be stored without excessive deterioration. Typically, there is usually a university requirement for an itemised list of all artefacts/outside items and/or non-book media to be included with the submission. This is useful for the assessors to help calculate and give feedback on what further work you might need to present to meet the expectations and requirements of your institution, and to be accepted for enrolment to write your synthesis when you have sufficient.

▶ Sufficiency of work for the PhD by published work (prospective route)

I surveyed a number of individuals who were undertaking a prospective route, exploring the number of papers they needed. Universities vary hugely on their sufficiency requirements for specific require/research outputs for the prospective routes they offer. On average, they required between five and 10 co-authored and/or sole-authored book chapters and papers in varying proportions. Some do not allow book chapters at all because of the lack of consistency in the peer-review process for some edited books. Some candidates had a clear institutional requirement to submit six papers over five years on one coherent theme from the point of registration but chose to submit additional sole-authored, peer-reviewed papers to strengthen their coherent body of work. You are in a lucky position if you can do this. Other

---

Insider Perspective 2.3 Sufficiency

Very often individuals just do not want to go through the conventional PhD as the thought of a formal research training programme in addition to writing an 80,000 word thesis simply deters them. This academic, currently undertaking a PhD by publication, describes to Draper (2012) what happened to him.

> Somehow, the pressure of not having a PhD led me to shop around for a PhD by published work. I decided to check out UK universities. Unfortunately, most UK universities only offer this type of degree to their own teaching members. Only a handful of new universities offer this route. When I first registered, I was rejected by three universities, one citing that my publications lacked 'newness' in terms of knowledge, another rejected without reasons, while the third felt that my publications were not 'good' enough, lacking a strong empirical dimension. So, two to three years later, now with more publications, I applied to the third university. And they accepted my application. I didn't have any published books at all to begin with, but I will be submitting twelve single authored refereed papers published mainly in UK mainstream journals.

prospective route candidates were required to submit with their curriculum vitae listings of all conferences attended and presentations they had undertaken relating the coherent research theme in the duration of the registration period. This indicated competence and activity as an independent active researcher. Only at that point was it agreed that it was representative of a coherent body of work. (See Insider Perspective 2.3.)

▶ Support from your university

Your doctoral study is a shared responsibility. Although many would argue that, at times, it seems the burden of the research, writing up and learning seems solely to be borne by the candidate themselves! However, your university should at least provide your frameworks, policies and regulations to set you up for success for your PhD. Within the university infrastructure lie research groups, faculty groups, supervisors and colleagues to advise who is responsible for establishing processes which can help contribute to your success. You are the central hub of all this but the experience is slightly different when doing a PhD by published work. A candidate undertaking a standard PhD will enrol and, after five or so years of research, using material and human resources, working with a supervisor over time, several redrafts and a viva will hopefully be successful in obtaining a PhD.

Undertaking a published work PhD means you will probably be accessing this 'material and human' support in different ways. If you are writing gradually, you will be working with different colleagues and groups over time on different projects. You may be more established in your university (if you are an existing member of staff) and may have a clearer knowledge of the research support, libraries and networks available to help you. You will undoubtedly have to attend the standard university research induction (this may, or may not, be tailored for PhD by published work students). This is an important part of the registration process and the sessions (together with your handbook) will outline the process, the hurdles, the underpinning regulations, and online and face-to-face support facilities available to you. However, most importantly (and considerably different from the conventional PhD student, or those on the prospective published work route), if you are taking the retrospective route you will only have a supervisor/advisor allocated in the year you enrol and are ready to finally write up your synthesis.

PhD students undertaking the traditional PhD route commonly need funding or a tenure to fund them through their studies. However, during my interviews and surveys of PhD by published work students, I heard many successful insider perspectives from candidates in the UK and abroad (usually employed university staff members) finding research grants to support their coherent theme, which allowed them to step back from their teaching commitments. There were also opportunities for six-month university sabbaticals and scholarly breaks granted for staff to write up their syntheses.

▶ The typical process of undertaking a PhD by published work

Very often universities *only* offer the PhD by publication routes to their own graduates or employees, so you should investigate the criteria and regulations for registering for this award at your specific employing university. In addition, sometimes it can take time to find a university course to suit you. University website details of research awards are not always accessible or open to external view. I made a basic internet search of 10 universities in the UK and 10 international universities. Only 50 per cent of the universities advertised the award to external potential candidates and, even then, the conventions and regulations were not always accessible on the website and contact had to be made through the University Research Office or its equivalent. Willis (2010) has described the difficulties of finding a published work route, describing it as a 'quite a quest' to obtain the necessary information. Issues about eligibility for enrolment, accessing and understanding the selection criteria, and information on the application process are the most problematic issues to navigate.

There will be a system designed to help support you to succeed and this will build in measures of accountability. At regular intervals, during your enrolment period your progress may be monitored and there is series of stepping stones to cross on this administrative and regulatory journey. For a PhD by publication (the retrospective route), you are usually only enrolled for one year as you write up your synthesis, (thus only paying one year's fees), so it is unlikely that you will be required to write progress reports and have these signed off at regular intervals. This is typically the practice for standard PhD students, or for those undertaking the published work prospective route. The UKCGE report (2004) commented on the wide range of fees charged for PhD awards across universities, reflecting 'the persisting wide range of interpretations of what the degree demands of candidates and academic staff.'

A general process pathway for all published work routes now follows. This will differ between universities.

Application

This varies across different universities and some have found the application process disorganized and laborious (Willis, 2010). It is now becoming more common for universities to have a pre-qualification stage post-application. Implicit in this stage is the idea that some kind of gate-keeping occurs before access to the full assessment is required (UKGCE, 2004). Most (86 per cent) of UK universities now have a two-stage submission: the first stage is designed to establish a *prima facie* case for the application (a list of publications completed – or planned, if the prospective route – and a short analysis of the contribution to knowledge made by them); the second stage consists of all the compiled publications themselves with or without an accompanying analysis (UKCGE, 2004).

Applicants for admission to a doctoral degree by the published work routes are selected with the same care as those embarking on the traditional route to a doctorate. For retrospective candidates, an initial assessment is made of the number of the papers offered and then a more detailed proposal post-application is written, to allow for assessment of the quality and coherence of the applicant's publications, and to judge whether the applicant's work is suitable for doctoral submission.

Other universities ask for a summarizing proposal to be submitted simultaneously with the application and this will also be examined by a university panel. This can be a lengthy process. Candidates will usually be invited into the university to explain their publications and research history. This often happens after the candidate expresses an interest in a PhD route by existing published work and prior to formal application. The panel (usually composed of internal senior professors and research advisors/supervisors, who are typically members of the university or faculty research committees) reviews whether the potential candidate could be supported in having a reasonable chance of a successful completion; that their peer-reviewed research is part of a larger body of work and is sufficient in quality, impact and quantity; and whether it has some clear thematic areas. Candidates for the prospective routes need to be able to show that their research work and planned papers and ideas are focused, rich and sufficiently promising to be completed successfully in the time allowed.

The UKCGE (2004) report outlines key areas for examiners at this stage, focusing on evaluating the contribution to knowledge of the candidate's published work, whether there is a satisfactory level of coherence between the publications, evaluating whether the candidate has contextualized and analysed their publications in any required critical appraisal, assess the candidate's contribution in terms of co-authoring and, thus, the sufficiency of the publications. At this stage, if there is lack of crucial evidence in the submitted publications themselves, this issue might at least be partially addressed within an accompanying critical appraisal document. This stage in the process is useful for the universities *and* the candidates. The process minimizes the chances of false expectations by the potential student, reduces the wasting of time in the future for both the supervising staff and the student by ironing out quality and quantity issues with publications, and strengthens the rigour of the research work submitted for awards at that particular university. Candidates are usually accepted or declined at that point. Those declined are usually given feedback to enable them to continue publishing in their particular themed area and are given guidance about the quantity/sufficiency required to be accepted for that university's award, so they can resubmit a pre-application at a later date.

Allocation and selection of the supervisor

The most influential form of support you receive as you write up your synthesis will be from your supervisor/Director of Studies (DoS)/advisor. Chapter 4 addresses the roles and responsibilities of the supervisor; needless to say, a good match is important. Let us explore the thorny issue of nomenclature and why the supervisor for a retrospective route is not really a supervisor but is, rather, an *advisor.*

If you are an internal candidate applying within your university for a specific PhD by published work, the university research office may ask you to suggest suitable individuals who could be your supervisor/advisor. If you are lucky enough to be in a position to choose your supervisor/advisor, then grab it with both hands – you will already know the expertise of staff in your university and who you can work with effectively (see Insider Perspective 2.4). An experienced supervisor/advisor with a good understanding of the PhD by published work process (retrospective or prospective), the paperwork and how to guide you in the writing of a good quality synthesis, is worth their weight in gold. Many of my interviewees described real difficulties in finding a supervisor who was familiar and confident in supervising published work routes. Most universities require that an individual undertaking a PhD by published work has two supervisors. One supervisor would be a Director of Studies (DoS), who takes primary responsibility for the meetings/coordinating the paperwork and activities. The other supervisor would have a complementary skill set and would have a good (if different) knowledge of your field; this enables them to offer feedback on synthesis drafts. Regulations usually specify that any supervisor should not be a main co-author on your publications. However, sometimes, if the subject field is narrow, it may be realistic to assume some supervisors may have been involved in co-writing (or part of the research team) for your earlier publications.

Insider Perspective 2.4 Choosing the advisor

I chose my supervisor (although they call them 'advisors' here because they don't supervise my research – that is done, dusted and quality-assured by the journal) who advises me with my synthesis because I was registered for my PhD by published work where I was (and still am) employed. I knew about the most suitable people to supervise me. I had two. One whom I met every couple of months, a specialist in the ethnographic and qualitative approaches I'd adopted for most of my published work, and the other came from a different discipline area but offered a fresh pair of eyes on my work and approach and content of my synthesis from a much broader perspective. They both read the drafts of my synthesis and sent comments not on the research itself which has already been peer-reviewed but on the visibility of the themes and the coherence.

Sarabjit, mid-career, PhD by published work (retrospective route)

Enrolment

Once accepted and enrolled (i.e. signed up officially as a registered student at the university of your choice), you will be able to access the research and library facilities at this point from your enrolling institution – that is, you will be able to view their databases, which host a wide range of publications. Your library will be able to offer you access to electronic and/or paper copies of the most recent articles. This will help you collate ideas for your synthesis and evaluate your older publications against newer literature. The libraries may also offer a mechanism for you to receive details or text alerts of the editions of your favourite journals. This can be useful if you are writing your synthesis to a coherent subject theme and you want to make sure your work can be elucidated and compared with the most recent material in your subject. In addition, you often can find your own work cited in later articles and this can be incorporated effectively into your synthesis or in the viva, where you may be asked about your contribution to the knowledge base and the impact of your work over a longer time frame.

A PhD by published work student planning to undertake the prospective route from scratch will usually enrol after their application has been accepted on a set date agreed mutually as the starting point for the registration period. You will have a supervisor identified at this time to support you through the planning and writing of your publications. However, it is likely that much of this informal planning work and discussion could be achieved prior to official enrolment, particularly if you are an internal staff member already undertaking research but not actually having written up any of your work for publication.

Confirmation of registration

If a university does not have a pre-qualification stage for acceptance on the award, then their regulations may include a milestone known as the 'Confirmation of Registration' (CoR) for published work routes (see Insider Perspective 2.5). This stage considers the proposed candidate's papers as reviewed by an academic panel of researchers and, usually, includes some form of viva or interview, depending on the university's regulations. Typically, candidates undertaking this PhD route will often have a confirmation of registration meeting four to six months after enrolling, the purpose of which is to check progress and to assess whether the candidate has any additional training needs. The review panel usually comprises the supervisor and senior members of research staff with experience of successful completions of the published work route. Typically, the candidate presents their publications and explains their theme. Quite often, universities will ask in advance for a 200–300 word summary of each paper/output, if this has not already been written for the earlier application phase (later, this will be appended to the submitted synthesis). The panel reviews these summaries and then usually addresses much the same issues as addressed at the pre-qualification stage:

* Will the submitted work realistically allow the candidate to achieve a PhD by published work? (Bear in mind, the existing/retrospective published work candidate will have enrolled only after proven publications sufficiency at the application stage.)
* Is the candidate aiming to enrol on the prospective route likely to be able to pursue the research project at that level and how are they progressing?

Insider Perspective 2.5 Confirmation of registration

I was doing it by existing published work and didn't have a pre-qualification stage. I had to submit a list of all my papers, the list I was submitting for the PhD, a CV, and a brief rationale for my key themes and a draft of a synthesis.

I then discussed all these documents with a panel of four. One of the members of the panel was my supervisor. He didn't chair the Confirmation of Registration meeting and didn't contribute but wrote action points and feedback which we discussed at a subsequent meeting. I received a letter a week later collating the panel's feedback on the synthesis. My supervisor and I then discussed it a subsequent meeting and integrated some of the actions into the content of my synthesis which was draft at that stage.

PhD by published work (retrospective route), UK

- Are there sufficient resources available to support this candidate in the university? Are the ethical considerations for the candidate's projects in place and are the proposed published works making them suitably explicit?
- Does the candidate have any additional training needs?

Supervision/advisor meetings

These meetings will occur regularly throughout your registration period. As discussed, the nature of 'supervision' differs depending on whether you are undertaking the award retrospectively or prospectively. The nature of the content of the meetings, building relationships with your advisors and advice about different models of supervision is explained in more detail in Chapter 5.

Submission of the synthesis

Typically, universities offer retrospective candidates between 12 and 18 months to submit their synthesis. Candidates for the prospective route usually submit their synthesis/reflective piece as an integral element to (but towards the end of) their period of registration. Extensions of these timescales are usually only granted for health and personal issues, but not for workload or time management issues. Many universities only offer their awards to existing internal staff members. While the limitations of this restrictive process have been addressed above, it does help to assure that the departments in which candidates are employed give sufficient time for scholarly work to those candidates to complete their synthesis in the allocated time, thereby minimizing the risk that workload can be given as grounds for mitigation. This might sound harsh but, in some ways, benefits the students. It ensures that they have sufficient staff development time, minimizes lengthy registration periods (and more fees), and recognizes that the body of the work (for retrospective candidates) is complete prior to enrolment, thus allowing adequate time for the completion of the synthesis. In practice, many of my interviewees from a range of different universities across the world described various levels of allocated hours for research, difficulties with work–life balance, and stress resulting from completing an academic award at the same time as undertaking their university teaching work.

▶ Insider perspectives: choosing the route

Insider Perspectives 2.6, 2.7 and 2.8 examine three different views about route choice. Different career stages, numbers of publications, life-stage and job role can all impact on the choice of your eventual pathway.

Insider Perspective 2.6 Choosing the route

What was my situation? This was the route that suited me. I had 15 publications over a 12-year writing period, not all of them were in a coherent subject area and not all in peer-reviewed journals. I had no book chapters at all, had some work that was co-authored, mostly single-authored. I had a love of writing and a desire to contribute to my area of academic interest (interprofessional learning and critical reflection).

By dint of some necessary culling, the addition of some peer-reviewed book chapters, I realized I had enough material to form a body of work which could at some point be refined into a synthesis and which I was able to defend in a viva. This retrospective review of my publications meant that I could enrol as I was ready to write my synthesis.

It cost a year's fees instead of five and allowed me a 'pause for thought' and an opportunity to consider my work as a cohesive, chronological body of academic activity. Success in a PhD by publication can enhance one's love of writing and not dampen it. It allowed parallel submissions of publications to the Research Excellent Framework and practice speaking about the subject area at conferences and in the classroom.

Susan Smith, mid-career, completed PhD by published work (retrospective route), UK

Insider Perspective 2.7 Choosing the route

I was a professor and had been for many years. I have supervised many people and the university wanted everyone to have a PhD, so it felt a bit strange not having one myself. I had over 20 papers and many books published so everything was in place before I registered. I didn't have to add anything I picked the most coherent theme from my writing of the last 10 years using two books, and seven published peer-review papers. The real challenges have been that I have only just started writing my synthesis as I have only just registered, university bureaucracy, and the difficulty in getting all the original pdf versions of the articles and papers from the journal editors. As I have supervised over 20 PhD students and 10 of these by the published work route, I need to take my own office but, in fact, my Director of Studies is the most helpful. I found it quite easy to find a coherent theme based around one element of my specific research area, and I only chose papers and articles and chapters that addressed the theme in a really focused way. I went for focus and good quality and resisted the temptation to go for quantity. It forces you to reflect on your body of work – strengths and weaknesses.

University Professor and Supervisor of PhD students (traditional route), UK

Insider Perspective 2.8 Choosing the route

What was good was that it was just not as public a route as doing a traditional PhD, and I undertook the writing up of many of my papers at the weekend or in the evenings without initially gaining permission of my line manager (who I felt might otherwise wish to over-direct the focus), I then began to undertake more, started presenting at pedagogic conferences as part of my day job and, in parallel, writing up journal articles for the Research Excellent Framework. Later, when I enrolled for my synthesis, my work was deployed and discussed as part of my annual appraisal.

Senior Lecturer, mid-career, PhD by published work (retrospective route), UK

▶ Activity

Try the following activity and look at the Appendix (pp. 143–8) for some examples that others have submitted.

Task: Choose the PhD by published work route to which you are most attracted. Look closely at the regulations for this award and, using Table 2.1, consider whether you are in a position to enrol now or in the future. Complete the table and be honest with yourself about the quality, coherence and number of publications. This will give you the most accurate picture of the current state of affairs and what you need to do to develop a complete portfolio of papers or artefacts for submission.

You could then take the completed table to your chosen University Research Office or a potential supervisor, academic mentor or colleague. Complete the actions box – it will help you summarize future goals.

Table 2.1 Publications/theme calculator

Where are you now? Are you en route to a PhD by published work?	Number of publications for submission and theme identification
Do you have a wider body of peer-reviewed work from which you can select some papers around a core theme(s)?	YES/NO
How many *single-authored papers* in peer-reviewed journals have you got in total?	
Are they all around a *core theme*?	YES/NO
How many have you got on a *core theme*?	
How many *joint-authored papers* in peer-reviewed journals?	

→

Where are you now? Are you en route to a PhD by published work?	Number of publications for submission and theme identification
Are they all around a *core theme?*	YES/NO
How many *joint-authored papers* have you got on a *core theme?*	
How many peer-reviewed book chapters have you got? Does your university count them?	
Are they all around a *core theme?*	
How many have you got on a *core theme?*	
Does your university allow conference papers, films, performance, exhibits, artefacts or teaching materials/ resources as part of the submission?	YES/NO
If YES, how many of these high-quality artefacts have you got?	
What's your current useful total?	Date:

How many more of each do you need?
  Papers
  Book chapters
  Other artefacts (conference papers, reviews, media, exhibits, learning resources – check your regulations for the allowance)	

You could give this form to an academic mentor/potential supervisor or colleague for advice and comment Supervisor's comments (please complete below)	
In the light of the comments above, what's your action plan? Can you set some achievable publishing goals with a colleague/mentor/potential supervisor?	

3 Writing for Publication and How to Maximize the Impact of your Publication Outputs

A PhD by published work involves ... publications. Whether you like it or not, (and somewhat obviously) the correct number of publications or outputs in academic journals and the public domain are the key to success on this route. You might be at the start of your prospective route seeking help on where to send your planned publications, or writing continuously anyway in the hope of submitting a retrospective collation of papers.

This chapter addresses how to improve your success rate in writing papers for journal publication. It discusses different ways of targeting journals; what counts as a publication; and how exhibitions, different forms of media, artefacts, and learning and teaching resources could contribute to the total of your submitted works. I will address how using peers, networks, communities of practice and journal clubs can enhance your confidence, speed up your submissions and, hopefully, influence your success rate. The chapter offers strategies for dealing with journal peer reviewers' comments, either individually or as a co-authoring team. The trials and tribulations of co-authoring and the practical elements of authors' respective contributions are discussed and illuminated by authentic examples from PhD by published work candidates. The chapter also addresses the thorny issue of choosing the best journals to target specifically for the purpose of gaining a PhD by published work. This includes consideration of the dilemma of whether to aim for top journals, which are more competitive and may slow down your acceptance rates (which may be problematic on a planned prospective route), or to settle for middle ranking/newer journals, which will potentially enable you to publish the required number of articles in a shorter time. The chapter concludes with a short piece on the value of writing a capstone article that helps to demonstrate the coherence of your case, and how the very act of writing the capstone article and finishing your papers and synthesis can generate ideas for future spin-off publications in new directions.

▶ Making the process and the task work for you

It makes sense to say that the key to success with your PhD by published work is actually getting published! Getting your precious fruit of your labours published in the right place to suit the right audience for your work and to count towards your award is absolutely critical.

Candidates undertaking a PhD by published work appear to have two key agendas: the first is that they genuinely want to strive to make a significant contribution to their field of knowledge and, in an ideal world, to disseminate pearls of wisdom to a worldwide audience in the form of eminent journal articles and books. However, this idealism is often compromised by the second agenda: the sheer, blatant necessity of needing to gain publications for an award that will, in time or in parallel, lead to getting a job in a university, or a better job in a different university, or be an essential prerequisite to a post or promotion. Academic staff are expected to write for publication, and (whether collated for a PhD or not) the steps involved to achieve a successful publication can still be a daunting task for many.

In particular, for anyone new to writing for publication, there are weighty pressures associated with both initiating and completing the process, and these challenges can hinder success. Smith and Deane (2014) have discussed the key barriers for new PhD students to writing theses and journal publications, and address the key issue as 'cognitive overload' – because so many skills have to be learnt simultaneously, which can hamper motivation. This increased emphasis on publications in the academic field will hopefully not result in the proliferation of sub-standard work but, rather, definitely contribute to a visible competition for 'journal space' in respected publications. In response to this, since 2010 there has been a marked increase in the number of research journals and outlets for potential publications.

If you do not have something to say in your proposed journal article that has not already been said many times, or you do not have research that is new and interesting in your field, or you do not have research results that are significant, then you probably will not get published (Sadler, 1992). So, before you even think about submitting, ask yourself whether your work is original, sufficiently interesting and fills a gap in the knowledge.

▶ The reality of publishing: PhD by published work (prospective and retrospective routes) – student experiences

Students undertaking a PhD by published work appear to be getting mixed messages – or, rather, they interpret them as mixed when the messages are probably necessarily and sensibly conflicting. Many of my survey respondents described how their supervisors encouraged them to go for high-quality journals, especially with co-authored work that reflected well and impacted on the authoring team. Others said they were actively encouraged to try for middle-ranking, new or open source journals with shorter review periods to expedite publication times. Some of the PhD by published work candidates and academic writers I spoke to discussed some of the issues relating to journal impact and choosing the right journal for your work. Most academic staff agree that aiming for the top journals with a high impact factor should be encouraged. However, competition for articles to be accepted in these journals is stiff and these journals often have a longer lead-in time for publication, which may affect candidates who need to collate a portfolio of published work in a specified time frame. As a result (especially for those undertaking a prospective award from scratch), many individuals are frank in their pragmatism and take the decision to aim for more generic middle-ranking journals so as to publish their papers as swiftly as possible. In addition, many passionately discussed their loathing of journal 'snobbery' but acknowledged the thrill of getting published in a prestigious journal. (See Insider Perspective 3.1.)

Insider Perspective 3.1 Choosing journals strategically

One of my international survey respondents, who has now completed his published work PhD, chose his journals strategically to support a new career direction.

> I wanted to move my career towards a more international focus and doing a PhD by publication gave me a way of gaining immediate international recognition by publishing my research. I specifically submitted my work to peer-reviewed international development journals because I knew the leaders in the international health field read those specific journals and I wanted to influence policy with my original work. I targeted journals which combined pharmacy, nursing, public health and focused on open access to enable global application. Publishing in the right journals was a successful way to transition into a new international career.

Academic, mid-career, completed PhD by published work (retrospective route)

Many researchers at an early stage in their careers actively target new, lower-impact, generic journals not only to speed up acceptance rates, but also to gain confidence and to experience the review process prior to submitting to higher-impact journals as sole authors. Others, with burgeoning research careers, work in a well-established research team and eventually become principal investigator or lead author for some of the papers (teams need to be clear about the percentage of writing contributions), submitting the co-authored work to the higher-ranking, specialist journals. This approach allows researchers to build confidence, work in a functioning and productive team of co-authors, split themes to generate more papers and eventually achieve their PhD by published work. This also allows those individuals undertaking the route prospectively to achieve sufficient publications in the desired time.

Others researchers only achieve their PhD by existing published work at the end of long illustrious academic writing careers, often choosing eight to 10 key papers from a much wider portfolio of work submitted to a full range of specialist, prestigious, established journals. These individuals often did not plan to be a candidate on a prospective route and were not in the position in their early careers to adopt a particularly strategic approach to journal submission. Often, when they become professors towards the middle and end of their careers because of the eminence and impact of their work, it is only then that they decide to collate their best papers for a PhD, often just prior to retirement.

Some subject areas had very few high-impact journals but researchers 'just knew' to which journals to submit their work because, in the sector, their influence and importance was well-known. For example, in my discussions with staff about publishing research into higher education pedagogy, they explained there are a limited number of high-impact journals and many new ones, but the participants aspired 'intuitively' to publish in *Assessment and Evaluation in Higher Education*. In our discussions, specifically in the subject area of research in higher or further education, they listed the following journals in which to publish teaching and learning related papers:

- *Assessment and Evaluation in Higher Education*
- *Higher Education*
- *Studies in Higher Education*
- *Innovations in Education and Teaching International*
- *Quality in Higher Education* (for policy issues)
- *Higher Education Quarterly* (for policy issues)
- *Active Learning in Higher Education*
- *Higher Education Research and Development*
- *Teaching in Higher Education*.

> **Insider Perspective 3.2 Choosing journals to suit your own timeline**
>
> Primarily, I have chosen journals within my sphere of practice and tried
> to ensure the articles fit within the journal aims and scope. I also
> thought a lot about the time taken to receive feedback and the likelihood
> of the paper being accepted. My university regulations mean the article
> can be included for my PhD publications submission just on acceptance
> (rather than actual full publication in the journal) for publication and this
> speeds up the process slightly. I gave some consideration to the ranking
> but my main aim was expediting the acceptance. This meant careful
> choices, chasing the journals and responding to required revisions very
> rapidly.
>
> **Anna, Principal Lecturer, mid-career, PhD by published work
> (prospective route), UK**

A common and useful practice is to use conferences and seminars to
strengthen work prior to seeking publication in a high-value journal. This
process facilitates the gauging of the interest from the discipline and generates views from expert colleagues about the currency and meaning of the
work. This can then provide true confidence in preparing to write for a
higher-impact journal. One of my colleagues (currently writing slowly and
collating papers for a retrospective award), described how she initially wrote
a paper for her special interest group at the UK Higher Education Academy,
then chose the best national and international conferences (in her case, the
Society for Research in Higher Education conference and the Conference of
the Higher Education Research and Development Society of Australasia),
presented her work, refined it in the light of issues raised constructively by
delegates at both conferences and then, finally, had it published in
Assessment and Evaluation in Higher Education. She was clear that the longer
time frame and a high-quality journal led to a better outcome and higher-
quality output than if she had 'compromised' on a middle-ranking paper (see
Insider Perspective 3.2). She also regarded compiling her portfolio of high-
quality publications as a long-term exercise and thinks it may take eight to
10 years to have sufficient high-quality papers to submit around a coherent
theme.

▶ Working with the regulations

Look carefully at your regulations and, if you are unclear about them, then
seek advice from the university. This will save time and effort in the future

as it is pointless working towards a published work award if you are producing the wrong type of written materials for the journals you identify, or are producing unsuitable artefacts for an exhibition, or are, in general, producing unsuitable outputs for the award on which you are enrolled. It is as bad as taking an examination and writing a superb answer but not answering the question as it has been framed.

What published work can you count?

Most university regulations stipulate the kind of published work which is acceptable for the count. The work must be traceable through catalogues, abstracts, citation indices or equivalent, and be publicly registered with an ISBN or ISSN number. A peer-reviewed element is essential, but not all articles have to be original research reports – some can be summaries of existing work, or a capstone article (see pp. 78–9) that perhaps encapsulates your chosen theme; scholarly criticism on a theme emergent from your existing publications may well also count. Critical reviews of artefacts, diverse media and resources also produced as part of a candidate's learning and teaching work may also count. Many universities consider different types of publications are appropriate for submission. For example, books and book chapters, monographs or other media in the public domain (e.g. architectural or engineering designs). Sometimes, the submission of a single book or artefact is also acceptable, with an additional commentary. In some arts fields, other works – such as installations, exhibitions, compositions, and performances – can be considered as part of the submitted portfolio of published work.

Many universities will have a cut-off period for publication to ensure currency. They will state that the body of work should not include any material produced, for example, more than 10 years before the date of submission. Retrospective candidates should check regulations: there may be the possibility that older papers which you thought might not be sufficiently recent can be counted. Alternatively, there might be the opportunity to write a new paper looking at more recent developments of the original work. The usual requirement is about six to 10 sole or first-authored papers published in high-quality, blind refereed, academic journals, supplemented by co-authored papers, chapters or research reports. Where multi-authored works are included, you are required to submit evidence of your individual contribution to the work.

In the case of other works in the arts, humanities and creative fields, these must have been performed, exhibited or published in the public domain and be subject to equivalent forms of critical review. As a standard guide in the UK, the published works should be recognized as being, *at least*, at the national standard in terms of the Research Excellence Framework

(REF) rating (or equivalent research assessment practice outside the UK). All published works must be in the public domain; manuscripts for works submitted for publication but not yet accepted are not eligible for submission. Any work which is not in the public domain – for example, a confidential research report – will not be eligible for submission for either a retrospective or prospective PhD by published work route.

A further key rule is that all the published works submitted *must* represent a coherent programme of research and make an original contribution to the present state of knowledge in your identified subject area.

Regulations and the book chapter: the thorny question

Some PhD by published work awards accept book chapters, others do not. This is not an issue about whether book chapters are of value but, rather, a comment on the intellectual quality control in respect of edited books, which can be variable as they are not always subject to peer review (Rugg and Petre, 2004). If they are subject to rigorous peer review, they may well be counted. The moral of this is that you should check your university's regulations carefully on whether book chapters are allowed as part of your submitted portfolio of work. This sounds ruthless but, if submitted book chapters are not counted for your award, you might be better off focusing your energies on writing the papers and producing the artefacts which will support the successful achievement of your award. If earning a PhD is your career priority, it is worth considering writing chapters as being less urgent and delay doing this until later in your career. Many colleagues incorporated the content of their successfully published papers into new book chapters once their PhDs were successfully attained.

► Practical advice for improving your success rate with journals

Choosing your journal

The *impact factor* of an academic journal is a measure reflecting the average number of citations of recent articles published in the journal. It is frequently used as a proxy for the relative importance of a journal within its field, with journals with higher-impact factors deemed to be the more important.

Impact factors are calculated annually, starting from 1975 for journals indexed in the *Journal Citation Reports*; however, they cannot be used to compare journals across disciplines.

Some journals may adopt certain editorial policies which might have the desired effect of increasing their impact factor. For example, some may publish large numbers of review articles which are generally cited much more than research reports of a single study. When choosing your journal, you should look out for requests made by a journal, or a publishing house, or from academic staff who may be collaborating through their networks, or who may be editing institutional journals and looking for *themed contributions*. If the invitation is related to your subject area, go for it! You can send some sample text to an editor who will read and check your work; they will be able to tell you whether it meets their threshold level, is sufficiently scholarly, and suits the aim and scope of the journal.

The internet and the advent of electronic journals has really changed the face of writing for journals. As paper prices have increased, so has the cost of printed journals and a plethora of electronic journal sites in every subject area have taken their place. Talking to individuals submitting for PhDs by publication, they felt that although the peer-review process for an electronic journal can be just as lengthy, very often your work can be disseminated to a much wider population – whereas paper journals are often necessarily only available to a more limited number of readers. It was clear they felt that the esteem attached to electronic journals was equivalent to traditional paper journals and it is fair to say that the academic community now regard them equally in terms of prestige. It is also important to bear in mind that peer-reviewed, open access journals are a very useful way to disseminate your work. It should also be remembered that there may be a fee for publishing in this sort of journal.

Being peer-reviewed

It may seem rather obvious but, if you are a candidate on the prospective route, before you start writing ensure your chosen journal has an ISBN number and a clear rigorous peer-review process with at least two academic referees (employed by that journal). It is quite clear that if you submit work that is too long, full of errors or that just does not suit the remit of the journal, it will not reach the peer-review stage.

How then can you maximize your chances of submitting a piece of publishable work? You can, of course, send any fully written papers off speculatively to a journal for review but this is a risky strategy. Minimize your risk by initially asking your supervisor's view on the suitability of the journal you may have selected. Read a few of the past editions. Do the contents pages of the existing editions float your boat? Can you see some thematic similarities? Does any of your work complement or add to the knowledge base advocated and published by the journal? It is also worth exploring whether these journals have invitations to themed issues, often announced one year in advance, into which you could tap. Many academics send emails to the journal editor with some sample text or a title to see whether the editor would welcome an article on the proposed subject area. It is worth finding out the name of the journal editor and make sure your covering email/letter outlines the scope of your project; summarizes your background and past publications; and (if relevant) mention the name of your supervisor, co-authors and research team.

Waiting for decisions

Once the peer reviewers have read an article, they will decide whether it will be accepted as it stands, rejected completely, or require revisions for tentative acceptance. Different journals have a range of different outcomes and the key thing to remember is that the whole process can be extremely lengthy. It is not unusual for a submitted article to need major amendments before it is finally accepted for publication by the journal ... so, be prepared to wait. Sometimes, the stage from proofed draft to a finished paper – involving with multiple edits and resubmissions, and then ultimate acceptance – can take up to eighteen months. If you have a tight timescale for your prospective route PhD by published work submission, then this is a factor that must be taken into consideration.

The more prestigious journals with the highest impact factor measures usually have the longest peer-review turnaround time, so be prepared for the long haul. The most prestigious journals often have a bank of finally accepted articles which then may wait for a future edition. Submitted articles outweigh the space available in which to publish them. Most PhD by published work award regulations allow papers that have been finally accepted for publication as 'countable'. If your paper goes into a bank of submitted papers with a 'Fully Accepted' stamp on it, and possibly with a date of the proposed edition, this will count as another notch in your bedpost on your PhD journey. In the meantime, carry on writing for your PhD by submitting articles to other journals. Do not wait to hear about one paper before getting on with the next (particularly, prospective candidates undertaking the work from scratch), otherwise your PhD timeline will fall behind schedule. As one of my interviewees said, you will spend a great deal of time twiddling your thumbs and 'waiting for something to happen and get really behind schedule'.

What's your market?

Every journal has its own particular strengths and preferences, and it is important for you to consider whether your work would be best published in a major academic journal or, if your work has practical and professional application, in a practitioners' journal. You should avoid writing up your research for publication in a vacuum – know where you are aiming to publish your work by carefully reviewing in advance the available outlets in your field.

Although it may sound rather Machiavellian, while you are writing your articles for academic dissemination try to think about your audience. Who is your target market? Is your work highly specialized in a discrete subject area? If this is the case, you may have to submit it to a highly specialized journal and, very often, you will be competing against more established authors who are older and more experienced, and who have established track records. Can you link to their research teams or submit jointly? Or, if not, and you need a single-authored piece to make up the number of your submitted papers, consider submitting a single-authored paper with a slightly different slant, or a reflective piece honed to be more suitable for a broader interdisciplinary or more general theoretical journal.

▶ Using others to build your skills: communities of practice

Relationships, identity and shared interests and repertoire

Communities of practice are formed by people who engage in a process of collective learning in a shared domain of human endeavour. In a nutshell, 'Communities of practice are groups of people who share a concern or a passion for something they do and learn how to do it better as they interact regularly' (Wenger, 2007). The theoretical concept of 'community of practice' has relevance for the research support networks established to help PhD students and, indeed, all academic staff who write for publication, or who are working on submitting other outputs (exhibitions, performances and so on) which will be located and critiqued in the public domain. The character- istics of such communities vary. Some communities of practice are planned and formal, others are very casual. However, members are brought together by joining in common activities and by 'what they have learned through their mutual engagement in these activities' (Wenger, 1998). For the purpose of this book, it is clear that an informal writing group for PhD students conforms to Wenger's definition of a community of practice.

A community of practice involves much more than the technical knowl- edge or skill associated with undertaking some task. Members are involved in a set of relationships over time (Wenger *et al.*, 2002) and communities develop around the topics that matter to people. The fact that they are organizing around some particular area of knowledge and/or activity (the PhD writing group, for example) gives members a sense of joint enterprise and identity. For a community of practice to function, it needs to generate and appropriate a shared repertoire of ideas, commitments and memories. It also needs to develop various resources, such as tools, documents, routines, vocabulary and symbols that in some way carry the accumulated knowledge of the community. In other words, it involves practice, different methods of undertaking and dealing with things that are shared to some significant extent among members. As Wenger indicates, the interactions involved, and the ability to undertake more complex activities and projects through cooperation, bind people together and help to facilitate the building of relationships.

Writing groups: generating your own community of practice for support

So, how can you apply Wenger's ideas to support you in your writing? Can you generate your own community of practice to help you and your colleagues achieve writing goals? Do you know others who are also on this route who are interested in sharing expertise and practice regarding their writing, research and subject areas? Do you have a shared commitment and interest in discussion and activities to improve your skills? Do you have the time to meet to develop strategies and tools and share practice in a joint enterprise to help each other? You could be well on your way to developing a new community of practice.

Paré (2010) has written about how the support of colleagues can be immensely helpful over time, particularly for those new to writing. He also considers that writing groups can be a useful means by which to enhance reflection on the process and content of emergent work, and reduce the high attrition rates by new academic writers to journals. Smith and Deane (2014) feel the high attrition rates among new writers is caused by their inexperience with structuring text, and the overwhelming perceived 'cognitive overload' generated by having to learn too many new skills simultaneously.

On investigation, support for PhD by published work candidates does seem to be extremely variable. Some candidates are lucky to have diligent supervisor/advisors and clear regulations, and belong to active research and writing groups. Others have an allocated supervisor/advisor who knows a great deal about the subject area but very little about the process of the route itself, and some feel they have little support – for the writing of their synthesis, in particular. It does seem, though, that peer mentoring and peer tutoring in small groups for academic writing has become much more commonplace, and a developing ethos of constructive support, draft sharing and new writing groups reflects this change.

New researchers who are starting out in the publication process and new PhD students may struggle with the art of writing, as they are often unaware of the strategies and skills to help them write well. O'Sullivan and Cleary (2014) discuss how students often focus on the product of writing, rather than engaging with the process of writing when often it is in the process of writing, and in the discovery of that process, that learning happens (Berlin, 1982; Emig, 1977). O' Sullivan and Cleary (2014) have described how their writing group at the University of Limerick, with a supportive model of student peer-tutoring based on Ryan and Zimerelli's (2006) model, encourages students to engage in their own writing and learning in a non-threatening, approachable and positive manner and has fostered a transformative learning environment with current co-creation of knowledge.

Smith and Deane (2014) explored how writing for publication could be a demanding and stressful experience from which there is 'no escape', as academics are supposed to write for publication as part of their job. They discuss how novice writers can best be supported by looking at promoting a writer's intrinsic motivation through collaborative writing (i.e. burden sharing and ownership) to reduce the new writer's stress and to foster publication success. They also write about how they used a favourite tool of academics, PowerPoint slides, as a way of building skill in structuring a potential paper for new writers in a group. The neophyte writers' cognitive overload is reduced as they use a familiar tool for a new purpose – moving text slides around to facilitate the ordering of information and structure of drafts. They discuss how this model, and its associated tools and ideas, could be usefully extrapolated to the running of writing groups for PhD students who are struggling with structuring papers for publication, or who are having difficulty engaging with the reflective writing process for the synthesis.

Examples of writing groups for PhD by publication

There are examples of informal writing groups for candidates of PhDs by published work for three years. These groups meet three or four times a year, nurture candidates and give them time to reflect, share ideas, and co-read and write with peers. They are residential meetings and, over the course of a weekend, offer time and space in which to share synergies, encourage interprofessional collaborations, and share and rewrite drafts in a supportive atmosphere. Members from a wide range of disciplinary backgrounds share concepts, references and approaches. The members also use these weekends to share information on their supervisory process, their confirmation of registration experience, to help each other with paper revisions and drafts, prepare for mock vivas, and foster a community of practice (often without knowing it!) of interdisciplinarity and shared practice. The weekends are tightly timetabled to maximize the use of the time. Other universities run

---

Insider Perspective 3.3 Establishing and running university writing support meetings

There were a few of us ... some academic staff had completed a standard PhD and were looking for help to turn the ideas in their research work into a book. Others wanted to write articles based on chapters in their thesis. Some were writing articles for their PhD by published work around set themes, and were having trouble planning their journal submissions and pulling their synthesis together. Despite the diverse needs of all these people (there were about 12 of us in all), we managed successfully to meet every eight weeks for two to three hours.

We allocated a chairperson who would put together a loose agenda of discussion points of content we wanted to discuss at the meeting. We were ruthless on time management, not letting one person hog the precious time. We had clear ground rules established at the first meeting. These included certain ways we agreed to give feedback and how we constructed the agenda. We all found it helpful. I had real difficulty planning the papers I wanted to write for my PhD by published work – I used to take draft plans to the meetings and we'd discuss them.

Writing group leaders and participants

---

informal writing groups. These may trigger collaboration in shared ideas to write for special edition journals around a particular theme to get new writers started, give peer critique on draft papers, and discuss the challenges and issues associated with writing. (See Insider Perspective 3.3.)

Various authors have reviewed how peer critique is very helpful for new writers. Kamler and Thomson (2006) have explored the emotional impact and value of writing groups in the process of becoming more 'writerly'. Caffarella and Barnett (2000) explored the experiences of 45 doctoral students, and found that preparing and receiving critiques was perceived to be the most influential element in helping them to understand the process of scholarly writing and in producing a better-written product. More specifically, these students believed that two key factors integral to the critiquing process were responsible for building their confidence as academic writers: personalized, face-to-face feedback within their writing group, and the iterative or ongoing nature of the critiques they received regularly at the meetings. In addition, these students emphasized that, although the critiquing process in the community of practice felt 'highly emotional' at times, it was a powerful tool in building their writing skills and habituating them to a review process.

Online forums are also useful (Maiden, 2013) and supervisors have also established draft reading support groups to assist a range of students undertaking a PhD by publication. These are usually outside the one-to-one supervision system but prove valuable as a subtle, supportive way of preparing students to write for publication in peer-reviewed journals (Kamler and Thomson, 2006). These are useful for sharing student drafts, working on planning journal articles, and sharing writing advice and ideas. Sometimes, they attract students from different disciplines and peers read each others' draft papers with the aim of simplifying language and cutting unnecessary jargon. The same peer support principle can be adopted for those in the arts field who may be building artefacts, making digital resources, or planning for an exhibition of their original work in the public domain.

The impact of publishing on the emotions

Writing is difficult. It is really hard work. Kamler and Thomson (2006) recognize the sheer labour and emotional impact the act of scholarly writing has on its proponent as part of the process of becoming confident and 'writerly'. Rugg and Petre (2004) take a positive approach in their discussion of the knock-on benefits of academic writing. They emphasize the need for author resilience and how the process itself transforms someone into 'a fully-fledged academic'. They discuss how the opportunity to engage in dialogue with peer reviewers provides a different experience from that involved in talking to research colleagues, or your PhD supervisor/advisor. The new insights and different perspective are valuable learning points and, through this critical exchange of ideas and the receipt of challenging feedback, this instrumental approach to publishing can shape thinking and creative ideas. On the down side, it can be a risky activity. Academic journals can act as gatekeepers to specific disciplines and are expected to be rigorous in the way they conduct their intellectual business (Thomson and Kamler, 2013; Watts, 2012). It is hard-going for the author (the risk is that they are tempted to give up) when most articles are rejected, with the majority that are published needing significant amendments before they are accepted. Candidates for a PhD must become resilient to this and work on avoiding any emergent cycle of deflation and lack of self-confidence which can be a side effect of multiple rejections. To counteract this, parallel strategies such as conference presentations and peer evaluation from other students can be a useful way of honing work prior to submission, preparing for a viva, building confidence and refining the scholarly voice on the PhD writing journey (Yates, 2010) (see Insider Perspective 3.4).

Very often candidates on a PhD by published work route are either publishing and working, or writing up their synthesis and working. Rather

---

Insider Perspective 3.4 Using colleagues in your field

I was writing up my synthesis on assessment to enhance learning and basically every time I went to teaching and e-learning conferences, here and occasionally overseas, I talked to people about advances in assessment, innovations, changes in the field and this kept my synthesis really current and contributed to the body of work that followed.

Rowena, Director, mid-career, completed PhD by published work (retrospective route), UK

---

like part-time students, they fit the doctorate in around competing priorities of paid work and family responsibilities and, sometimes, the opportunities to engage with other students on the same route can be limited. Linking to your research community and other colleagues is a beneficial approach to fostering confidence and resilience, and prevents the 'intellectual and social isolation' common in sole researchers, those who write without a co-author, and those who may be atypical or part-time research students (Taylor, 2002: 137).

To achieve a PhD by publication successfully, you need to write and *feel able* to write the journal articles and the synthesis. Murray (2013) discusses the pressure for increasing our publication output in higher education, the need to develop productive writing behaviours and the need to change some more negatively perceived writing behaviours in order to become more productive.

It is the *key* skill but, sometimes, scholarly writing can be a real struggle and, as I have mentioned before, really hard work. Donnelly (2014) has shown how increasing self-efficacy, class community, and peer feedback can all reduce writing apprehension and build confidence in terms of participants' critical writing skills. A study by Arkoudis and Tran (2010) revealed that academic writing within the disciplines is still largely an individual endeavour, and that more collaborative activity and draft sharing in writing groups as communities of practice would reduce apprehension about writing. Individual personal growth and intellectual development can be enhanced by being immersed in the research culture of the university and there is much to be said about being around other people who are actively engaged in similar work. Use the enthusiasm of others about new development in the field to help contribute to your synthesis. Staff undertaking a PhD by published work addressed and collated practical advice and tips for good writing, addressing the challenges and process of writing for publication (see Advice from Experience 3.1).

Advice from Experience 3.1
Practical tips for writing academic publications

- Environment: Choose the environments that best suit your ability to write. This could be at home on the dining table, or in the office, or library – choose the area that stimulates your creative juices.
- Use the time to best suit your mood: if you sit down and are not in the mood to be creative and it doesn't feel like 'writing time', then do something else related to the paper – spell-checking, looking at the structure, checking the data or references. Often, completing a few of the more mundane tasks first can get you 'in the mood' for more substantial writing activity.
- Save those gems! Jot down the 'ah ha' moments in notebooks, or onto the notes page on your mobile phone.
- Meet those deadlines: be ruthless about meeting them, or you will get behind schedule. Plan them to a preparation timeline to which you adhere.
- Perform that piece: work on your readability and flow by reading your paper aloud. Imagine you are presenting it at a conference. You are then able to hear whether the language feels natural and whether the overall piece feels suitably structured.

Presenting your work

Articulating your research is guaranteed to develop presenting skills and generate external interest in your work. It is helpful to continue this as much as you can throughout your writing and research career. I found this particularly useful in the year I wrote my synthesis. Seminar presentations, analysing and articulating similar papers at journal clubs and discussions on particular areas of your work can help you check whether your views are up-to-date, solve problems creatively, and help you to assess how original your work really is. This will help you evaluate how the combined weight of all your papers and accumulated work is contributing to the current state of the body of knowledge. Sometimes, audiences at conferences can be surprising, offering counter-arguments, questioning your views and challenging you. Again, this kind of debate should help you reflect on the approach you take with the content and direction of your emergent synthesis.

▶ Working with co-authors

The growth of co-authorship

The Bologna Process extols the importance of interdisciplinary research and this has naturally led overall to more co-authoring (Keeling, 2006). The Finch Report (2012) examined how to expand access to the peer-reviewed publications arising from the increasing research and publications undertaken across the world. It reported on how the numbers of published articles are on the rise globally, especially in high-growth countries such as India and Brazil. There is also growth in the number of new journals to support this rise and parallel expansion of collaborative research, which then naturally leads to more co-authorship. UK researchers are also more likely than those in almost any other major research nation to collaborate with colleagues overseas. Indeed, over half of the articles published by UK authors in 2013 included a non-UK author. This is not unique to the UK but is mirrored by major partners in Europe and America. An increase in domestic and international collaboration, and partnerships and co-authoring (particularly in science-related areas where collaboration is the norm) has been noted, too, through analysis of bibliometric data (Adams, 2013). In addition, there is some evidence to show that co-authorship leads to a higher number of citations (Bastow *et al.*, 2014).

The benefits and challenges of co-authorship

However, discussing co-authoring is akin to opening a can of worms. Approaches differ considerably across universities and different countries, and culturally specific views about the nature and interpretation of collaboration operate differently across disciplines. You will undoubtedly be familiar with the custom and practice in your discipline area and will have adapted to their mores. There are international agreements – for example, the Vancouver Protocol (ICMJE, 2013), which determines who should be named as an author as opposed to who should be thanked in acknowledgements only. Even the order of authors has been regulated. That aside, co-authorship is becoming more and more common. If you are undertaking a PhD by published work, co-authored papers can be submitted for your award portfolio but clarity over the proportion of your own contribution to the research and the output is important. It is important to check university regulations for your specific PhD route to check what is acceptable in terms of the numbers, balance and weighting of single- to co-authored papers for your submission. They vary considerably and you must ensure the credit proportions are correct when you submit.

You might actively want a co-author, if you are in the early stages of a writing career. A more experienced author (whether they are part of your research team or not) might help you with academic writing and be better at placing articles and sharing the work. However, Delasalle and Goodall (2013), at the University of Warwick, state that co-authorship might not necessarily be a good idea, if you want to enter the Research Excellence Framework in the UK (or the equivalent research assessment exercises, internationally) and not share the prestige, particularly if you actually prefer to work and write on your own. For example, the guidelines for the inclusion of co-authored articles in the REF 2014 submission state that, within the same unit, only one of you can put the publication forward for the REF, so this needs to be discussed and approved by your writing/research team. Delasalle and Goodall (2013) advise caution when working with academics with whom you may be unfamiliar. They also address the thorny issue that 'there is no such thing as equality of load' – as it is unlikely you will *all* do exactly the same amount of work on a paper. They emphasize that role clarity in the writing team for each paper/output is essential. This ensures fairness – the maximization of skill mix and usage is essential to ensure that, ultimately, all of the writing team count as authors.

There has been some debate, particularly on some research student blogs (e.g. thesiswhisperer.com), about the acceptable number of inclusions of co-authored papers in PhD by published work submission. The usual emphasis in regulations is on a greater proportion of texts that are single-authored, rather than co-authored. It appears that some examiners would be keen to see the proportion of co-authored texts increased, recognizing that the conceit of the 'solo author' is one of the main flaws of the traditional PhD. Demonstrating that you can work well with others is a key part of being an effective researcher. However, there is a balance to be found. Examining a portfolio of papers exclusively comprising joint papers would question how independent a candidate was and (even with co-authors' verifications of an individual's contributions), without some sole-written papers, it is hard to judge the individual candidate's own original contribution to a body of knowledge. However, it is clear that in science-related subject specialisms, sole-authored papers are rare, as most work is done collaboratively in larger teams. This means that most papers will be co-authored and this should be expected in the submitted portfolio of work. Examiners can and will explore the individual's personal contribution to the collaborative papers in the viva voce, questioning deeply and specifically on this.

Authorship credit

The Vancouver Protocol is internationally recognized as the standard for determining authorship on publications. It was first described by the

International Committee of Medical Journal Editors and is now applied across all disciplines in the world's top universities.

The updated Vancouver protocols (ICMJE, 2013) for co-authorship state that authorship credit should be based on all of the following criteria:

- substantial contributions to conception and design, acquisition of data, or analysis and interpretation of data; and
- drafting the article or revising it critically for important intellectual content; and
- final approval of the version to be published.

The Vancouver Protocol is also clear that all co-authors should be able to defend the paper (though not all the technical aspects).

It is important to note the 'and's here. It is not enough to have achieved just one or two of these criteria – a legitimate author would need to be involved in all three to be acknowledged as an author.

Some journals require statements of contribution. This is now increasing as a transparent way to validate contributions and ensure consistency of declaration from large co-authoring teams. For example, *The Lancet* makes the following request: 'We ask all authors and all contributors to specify their individual contributions at the end of the text. Please insert here the contribution each author made to the manuscript – e.g. the literature search, figures, study design, data collection, data analysis, data interpretation, writing, etc. If all authors contributed equally, please state this. The information provided here must match the contributors' statement in the manuscript.' These statements can be very helpful to you when you submit your portfolio of papers on application (if undertaking the award retrospectively), or on final submission (for the prospective route candidates).

How does co-authorship begin?

You might be working as part of a larger research team or have a joint planned research project with another academic colleague, having secured funding or noted a gap in the research. Sometimes, younger career academics can be writing up a meta-analysis or a literature review and ask for help from a more senior, experienced colleague who then helps with the design of the review, the analysis and interpretation of the data, and the drafting of the paper. This can be either in a formal, supervisory way, or as an informal arrangement. However, whatever the context, it is still important to consider whether that more experienced person then becomes a co-author (if they have met the Vancouver criteria), or should simply be acknowledged. PhD supervisors on the traditional route often co-author with their students. This may not be a reality for you if you are undertaking a PhD by published work. However, you may be part of project teams with other academics who (even if they are not your formal allocated supervisor) may act as co-authors of the paper. The important issue, as several of my interviewees said, is to have *clarity on relative roles of authors from the outset.*

Ordering of the authors

Approaches for author ordering vary. The first author can be decided by discipline – the head of department or professor usually goes first or last. This first author is regarded as the 'Senior Author'. Sometimes the order is decided by who is the Principal Investigator, or the named corresponding author for the research. Occasionally, author attribution is alphabetical (or reverse alphabetical). This approach is declining in science but still used commonly used in the fields of maths and economics. Sometimes, author ordering is decided (more problematically) according to who undertook the most work. Failure to agree authorship renders the paper unpublishable, so it is worth clarifying your approach at the beginning. Some experienced authors suggest new authors are named first and are generous in acknowledging the relative contributions of co-authors. You should also use listed acknowledgements for those that have 'contributed' or 'advised' but who may not have satisfied the three elements of the Vancouver criteria.

Different experiences of co-authorship

Co-authoring is not only the modus operandi of large research teams. Smaller, single institution research teams can be a practical and effective way to write (see Insider Perspective 3.5).

Goodall (in Delasalle and Goodall, 2013) describes her approach to co-authorship as a form of shared research where papers go back and forth and where everyone has their own expertise. Sometimes, small teams of researchers work together and co-design projects using mixed methodologies. They submit publications to a range of journals which might attract qualitative or quantitative approaches, analysing the information in teams, some analysing the statistics, others undertaking thematic content analysis – but all commenting and working on the drafts as they develop. Other team approaches to might be established for those candidates writing for a prospective award as part of a team of co-authors. Many universities (because most papers in a science field are collaborative) do not specify a sole-/co-authoring requirement for papers submitted for prospective route awards for PhD by published work. Sometimes, a candidate's supervisory panel agree on a percentage allocation. A total of 100 percentage points are

---

Insider Perspective 3.5 Co-authors

The maximum number of co-authors I have ever worked with is five. This is a reflection of the smaller scale projects I have been involved in. Most of these were single institution projects where we collaborated in small interdepartmental teams to explore educational behaviours and perspectives. A larger research team wasn't necessary to accomplish the objectives of our work. I worked once on a project with one other author who then moved to another university and we were clear on our attributions to the papers prior to her departure. When we wrote up two papers about different findings from one research project having designed the project, interpreted the data jointly and shared and revised drafts iteratively, we decided at the beginning to take a 50/50 share in both papers from the beginning. When I used one of the papers for my PhD submission, she wrote me a supporting letter reflecting this prearrangement. There was never any trouble because we were upfront about it all at the beginning.

Sarah, Academic, mid-career, nearing completion of PhD by published work (retrospective route), UK

---

allocated per paper across the agreed authors. This percentage allocation takes into account the research needed and the development of the paper itself. This approach ensures author contribution is clear from the start with the view that, if circumstances change over the period of the prospective award, there is some discretion for modifying the percentage allocation. Sometimes, examiners may seek more clarification, provided in the form of a summary table that not only gives the percentages, but also providing a relatively brief narrative about the percentage allocations and the process for each paper. In addition, signed letters from the co-authors would be required to accompany the submission.

How to best work with co-authors

Carefully picking your co-authors can lead to a fruitful and long-lasting writing career. Individuals can work to their strengths and make optimal use of each other's research, analytical and writing skills. Co-reading of data, transcripts and statistics can enhance accuracy. Often, the naming of an allocated lead that coordinates the management of the paper submission works well, with a named person then taking responsibility for the initial structuring of the draft, and joint responsibility for interpretation, conclusions and recommendations. Meetings can be established to discuss analysis, interpretation, key structural points and the critical review of the conclusions and recommendations for future work.

It is vital to agree writing parameters if you are co-authoring. For example, allocated roles, the audience for your paper(s), the style of your journal and how that may or may not suit the skills of the writing team, agreed deadlines, agreed slippage time and what your process will be for addressing the paper's drafts (face-to-face, in sequence, or together through a collective 'track changes' approach).

Having sequential drafts to avoid confusion is usually best – that is, the identified 'lead' author generates an agreed draft cascade order so everyone makes their amendments in turn, rather than simultaneously within a specified window. However, sometimes in the early stages, when output ideas might be being discussed online, it can be useful to use a shared, mutually accessible document (e.g. Google docs) to undertake changes and make comments openly, so others can see what the comments are as they review it, too. This enhances transparency and rigour, and can expedite draft turnaround time. The concept of the order and structure of co-written papers for published work needs to be discussed by the authors. Writing an article does not mean you necessarily have to start at the beginning and then complete it systematically. You can each take different sections, often writing the conclusion first and the introduction last.

It must also be said that it is important to recognize whether co-authoring is not appropriate for you. If you prefer to write and work alone, then so be it – but, if you are not a naturally collaborative worker, bear in mind the risks attached to isolating yourself from academic practice and the value of having colleagues to act as critical friends and draft readers. Advice from Experience 3.2 summarizes views from academics with experience of writing as co-authors for publication.

Co-authors and the whole final submission

You will be asked by the university to list the relative contribution of your co-authors on the papers you submit with your synthesis at the end of the process. This must be prepared accurately. You should use some kind of template or pro forma to ensure that the relative contribution of each author is defined. In addition, it is also good practice to make sure that these contributions are authenticated through the co-author's feedback on headed notepaper, rather than by email, as it formalizes the process. Often, the order of the authors is not a good indicator of percentage contribution, with much of the hard research and data analysis being completed by the second-, third-, or fourth-named individuals on the list.

It is common sense that, if you are seeking formal relative contribution letters from co-researchers from an early paper in your research career, you should leave plenty of time to achieve this, as tracing individuals can

Advice from Experience 3.2
Smoothing the co-authorship path

- Regard co-authorship as professional practice and treat it in the same professional manner as you treat the rest of your work. One of my respondents described it as 'fraught with potential for resentment and one can walk into a minefield of competing or wounded egos – to apportion the responsibilities equally and be ethical in acknowledgement is hard, contested, territory'.
- Make no assumptions, have everything clear in terms of attribution at the beginning – you will do X and I will do Y. Decide whether someone will be the coordinator and drive the process (usually the principal investigator, who will then be the first listed author).
- Have clear deadlines – 'I will send you the draft of this by xxx and you will read it and get it back to me by xxx.'
- Accept that any co-authored paper takes longer to produce than a single-authored one, as you have to wait for all authors to contribute to successive drafts.
- Do not proof read and write at the same time. Do your writing and critical thinking first.
- Recognize your own writing skills and weaknesses, and delegate accordingly.

sometimes be a lengthy process. Copies of the authentication letters are usually appended to the final submission of your work for consideration by the examining committee. If you are a retrospective candidate using your existing published work, you may have to submit your co-authors' authentication to the Applications Panel initially (and before the last year, when you are writing up your synthesis). This validates the work early in the process and then frees you to write up your synthesis knowing your submitted papers have been approved.

▶ Dealing effectively with comments from reviewers

The publication of articles in any discipline is a complex and step-wise process that will, almost without exception, involve responding to referees' comments. If it is any comfort, it remains a hotly debated issue whether peer review really does help to differentiate between bad and good research, or whether it simply improves the readability and quality of accepted papers (Jefferson *et al.*, 2002). That said, however, dealing successfully with reviewers' comments can maximize the chance of acceptance and, if your aim is an award that centralizes publications, then it is probably reasonable to say you should abide by the rules of the game.

Williams (2004), in a literature review and a review of his own wide experience as a writer and journal referee, suggests a sensible, structured layout for responding to reviewers' comments including three golden rules: responding completely, responding politely, and responding with evidence. He also discusses the importance of resubmitting to the same journal if the comments are fair, rather than impulsively changing tack and submitting to a different journal in the same subject area in the hope that it will be accepted. Williams explains how authors need to be aware that, in some specialist research fields, work is likely to end up with the same referee when authors send their paper to another major speciality journal. It is quite likely that it would not go down well with that referee if they see the authors have completely ignored the referee's previous comments and have simply modified text to suit the requirements of a new journal.

Decisions, decisions
There can be lengthy delays from submission to receiving reviewer responses. (See Box 3.1.) Multiple revision cycles take time, so it is worth tackling all the revisions head on as soon as possible. Sometimes, particularly if you are writing for a specialized subject area, suitable reviewers can be difficult to find. This can be frustrating. Online tracking systems for papers are useful for keeping an eye on progress; however, you should chase the paper's progress up in person, if you suspect everything may have ground to a halt. If you are lucky enough to have your paper suitably reviewed, you will usually receive a letter from the editor with one of the following decisions about your paper.

Box 3.1   Decisions about papers (based on Williams, 2004)

Decision	Action for you and/or your co-authors
Accept with no changes	This is rare – usually only for commissioned reviews. Drink champagne!

→

Decision	Action for you and/or your co-authors
Accept with minor revisions	If you are the sole author, get on with these quickly. If you are working with co-authors, allocate a 'revisions coordinator' (as we called them) and try to agree to the revisions quickly so that they reach the editor by the date expected. If you send the revised paper back to the editor quickly, it is still likely to be fresh in his or her mind and you will achieve a rapid acceptance.
Major revisions needed	This is common. Read and reply to each comment in turn, following the layout and including Williams' three golden rules (p. 72) in each of them. This can take time. All authors must agree to revisions. Split up the sections/comments between co-authors, if necessary. Put in the necessary time to resubmit the paper to the original journal along the lines suggested. If it is a single-authored paper and you want it as part of your PhD by published work portfolio, then it is in your interests to get on with it swiftly.
Journal requests complete rewrite	This is tricky. Only you and your collaborators can decide whether the effort of a complete rewrite is worthwhile. Talk to the editor. Sometimes, they request that a paper is split into two, but there is still no guarantee that both will be accepted. If the referees' comments are supportive and the editor is keen, then it is worth considering redrafting the original paper. Before you begin rewriting an article, check with the editor that they would be willing to publish it and the proposed content. This approach might avoid this scenario occurring in the first place.
Outright rejection	This offers no opportunity to resubmit to the journal. Outright rejection is usually because the manuscript is unsuitable for the journal, or because of major methodological concerns raised by the reviewers. You will have to resubmit to a more appropriate journal elsewhere, correcting the flaws before you do so. If you feel the reviewers' comments are wrong (and, indeed, reviewers are humans and do make mistakes), you have the right to appeal to the editor. These appeals are rarely successful, especially if the editor trusts an experienced panel of reviewers.

Gilliver (2013) – an experienced science writer, research blogger and editor – supports this approach. In a conference presentation to early career researchers, he explored the best ways to deal with reviewers and I have used his advice below, and modified it using the views of my interviewees, colleagues and co-authors.

Use the reviewer comments even if your paper is rejected

Your paper getting sent out for review is a cause for celebration – not only because it might get accepted for publication, (and thus contribute to your growing PhD paper portfolio), but also because, even if it is rejected you, should at least get some feedback from the reviewers. When you receive your reviewers' comments, especially if they are lengthy and detailed, then try to overcome any feelings of personal attack and, instead, concentrate on addressing referees' concerns in a polite, objective and evidence-based way. You need to treat this stage of your work in the same way you treated the initial research and drafting of the paper. Each comment must have a polite, reasoned response to which all co-authors must agree.

Check through the reviewer comments carefully for things you can do to improve your paper before you decide whether to revise it, or to send it to another journal. Consider why you chose that journal initially. If the referees have not rejected it outright and have agreed to publish with revisions, it is almost always quicker and easier to stick with the original course of action. If referees are clearly saying that your paper is not suitable for the journal, then resubmit elsewhere. Speaking to two successful PhD by published work candidates, they described how they had each had papers completely rejected by one journal, improved their work with the help of the reviewer comments, submitted it to a better choice journal with a higher impact factor, and had it accepted there. If you are working with experienced co-authors, then it is likely that they will, between them, have a better understanding of which journals are most suitable for submission – that is, the chances of you sending a co-authored paper to a completely unsuitable journal are much reduced.

Be polite – but not over-polite!

It is fine to disagree with the comments of the reviewers but ensure that you address the reviewers politely, even if you totally disagree with them. However, you should not be over-polite. Gilliver (2013) once edited a point-by-point response to a set of reviewer comments in which the author prefaced and ended each individual response with an expression of gratitude: 'Thank you very much for your excellent comment. [Response to specific comment] Thank you very much again.' This excessive politeness might give the impression that the author is trying to charm the reviewer, to get the paper accepted by being polite rather than by addressing what the reviewers consider to be its flaws.

You and your co-authors do not have to accept everything the reviewer says

Responding to reviewer comments is a balance between satisfying the reviewer and editor, genuinely improving the paper, and being proud of the final output. If you accept all the reviewer comments and recommendations, you may increase your chances of publication but the paper might not necessarily be how you would like it to be. If you do not agree with something a reviewer says, you should say so, explaining your view (and those of your co-authors, if applicable) with clear reasoning. Colleagues of mine who are peer reviewers state that they respect authors who argue logically and cogently for their point of view. Remember, too, that accepting all of the reviewers' comments/changes still does not guarantee that your paper will be accepted.

Using evidence

If you disagree with a reviewer's comments, do not simply write 'I disagree.' Support your defence with a coherent argument and back it up with some evidence supported by references you can cite in your reply. Sometimes, you should add these references to the article itself, rather than only in the covering letter, addressing each of the comments in turn. Occasionally, there is no clear data to underpin your chosen methodological approaches; you should discuss this with an expert colleague in the field. If he or she agrees with your approach, you can state this in your reply to the reviewers. For example, 'Although different evaluative approaches and methodologies have been used in the past [*cite ref*], we have discussed this approach with Professor XX who wrote in [*name the paper*] and who agreed this could be an appropriate analysis ...' In reality, though, we do not always have access to the international expert in the field, or to an eminent professor who has written the seminal text in the area – and, indeed, often do not wish to bring colleagues into reviewer–author debates anyway.

What to do when two reviewers ask for opposite things and you only agree with one of them

This can happen quite frequently and you can end up fearing that you will ostracize one of the reviewers and put your chance of having your paper published at risk. One reviewer might think the methodological section lacks detail; the other might state that it was too convoluted, and should be briefer and clearer. You may have an instinct that one or other is probably correct. Whether it is co-authored or single-authored, it is worth initially seeking advice from more experienced colleagues or your co-researchers, who may well have a useful view. Then it is wise, if you are still unclear, to contact the journal's editor prior to responding to the revisions. Sometimes, it is worthwhile looking at other methodological sections of recent, similar papers published in the journal and modelling your response on that. In your response to the reviewers, you should explain clearly what you have done particularly in relation to which of the comments you have addressed and, if you have not addressed some, why this is so.

Gilliver (2013) also suggests that the author can then refer to the advice you received from the editor when writing your responses to the conflicting reviewer comments. Ultimately, it is the editor that has the final say on whether the paper is published.

Make sure you address everything that the reviewer mentions – do not pretend you have not seen what they have said

Sometimes, reviewers will raise several different points in a single comment. In such instances, it is easy to miss something important (or something that the reviewer considers important). Sometimes, addressing a series of hefty points made by a reviewer can be daunting – do not ignore them just because they seem insurmountable. Before you submit your responses to the reviewer comments, make sure you have addressed everything. Speaking to two colleagues who are peer reviewers of submitted journal articles, they expressed real irritation when authors fail to address all their comments. While recognizing an author might not agree with what they said, they acknowledge that they want each of their comments considered 'as a minimum'. When I was the lead author on a jointly authored article, we divided up the sections for each to address all the comments in that section. Using track changes and cross-checking, we would ensure as a writing team that not one single comment was missed. Ultimately, this strategy saved us time. The reviewers will keep notes of their tracked comments and, if you do not address their points the first time, around they will ask for the revision again. This simply delays publication – so you might as well get on with it in the first round of revisions.

Dealing with comments that perplex you

Sometimes, peer reviewers will make comments that you do not understand; on other occasions, it may be unclear whether they are merely commenting on something, or actually want you to make changes. When this happens, most people advocate a policy of openness. Explain to the reviewer that you do not understand what they mean, or what they are asking you to do. At the same time, it is worth writing responses based on what you suspect the reviewer may be getting at:

I am afraid that I am unclear about the point you are making. If you are saying that the sample was too small, I would respond that ... If, instead, you feel that the methodology was flawed, I would argue that ...

Engage the editor as an adjudicator

Gilliver (2013) suggests a course of action, if you (or you and your co-authors) and a reviewer are unable to agree on a particular point. If a reviewer repeatedly asks for a specific change and you reiterate your opposition to it and, after several rounds of the review process, consensus is no nearer, then in such circumstances it is advisable to address the disputed point directly with the editor. Present your argument to them as convincingly as you can and let them decide what should be done. He writes pragmatically, 'There is no guarantee that you will get the outcome you hope for, but at least you will no longer be bashing your head against a brick wall.'

Advice from Experience 3.3
Satisfying reviewers and editors and
successfully getting your work into a journal

In general, reviewers look for:

- Appropriateness to the journal.
- Clarity in expressing ideas the readers might want to know and understand.
- A good writing style.
- A thorough approach to treating the topic with rigorous and appropriate research methodology.
- Generalizability and validity of the findings/results.
- A unique contribution – that is, something 'new'.
- The importance of the subject.
- Timeliness and currency of the topic.

In general, editors look for:

- Appropriateness to the journal, and is it interesting for the readers?
- Clarity in expressing ideas for the readers to understand.
- Evidence the author has followed the journal guidelines for presentation/ format/words/referencing/tables/figures.
- Rigorous, appropriate and accurate methodology, statistics, literature review.

The advice in Advice from Experience 3.3 is based on the work of Professors Sally Brown and Phil Race.

▶ Writing a capstone paper

A capstone paper summarizes the essence of your core research theme. These are not a compulsory part of the PhD by publication process, but they can be very useful in clarifying your thinking, pulling together core ideas and addressing new literature which is not in your synthesis. Prospective route candidates often wish they had thought about planning to write a capstone paper when they were working initially with their supervisors to formulate the approach, profile and timelines for their publication.

Why do it?

As you start writing your synthesis, you are probably in a position where you have 'almost enough' sole- and joint-authored papers around a coherent theme to submit your work. At this point, many candidates choose to write their last paper in the form of a 'capstone paper' – that is, writing a sole-authored paper directed for a specific peer-reviewed publication which covers the essence of your core thematic content. It is vitally important that the content of any capstone paper *must be sufficiently different* from your synthesis, as it would be misleading and wrong to double-count your published outputs. However, quite often (and predictably) there will be some overlap of your literature and references; however, the direction of the capstone and the synthesis are – and should be – different.

Your synthesis (see Chapter 4) has to encapsulate the development of your 'golden thread', how each submitted paper addresses your key theme and clearly demonstrates the originality of all your work and its overall contribution to the knowledge in your research/subject area. In contrast, a capstone paper will be written towards the end of the publications journey (often, in parallel with the synthesis) and may (in contrast to the content of the synthesis) take a key element of one of the earlier papers and analyse it in more detail; include more current literature in more detail and point to new areas of practice in the light of your newer work and knowledge; and explore how it may have been transferred into other subject areas, and identify and critically evaluate possible future work streams in detail.

Not everyone may need to write a capstone paper. If you have sufficient sole- and joint-authored papers to meet the regulatory requirements and, with the completion of your synthesis, will have enough to meet the university's regulatory requirements, then it may not be necessary. Other candidates found that, when they had assembled their list of publications, they did not have enough to meet their university's requirements. One academic undertaking a retrospective published work route wanted to write a piece that 'acted as a real full stop to studies and serves a further purpose as acting as another peer-reviewed single authored paper.' The capstone paper addressed this need.

Advantages of writing a capstone paper

Many academics submitting for a published work route write their final capstone paper at the same time as they start to plan their synthesis. Sometimes, some of the synthesis ideas stimulated the content of the capstone paper and vice versa. The iterative process of writing the capstone paper helped to refine the content and focus of the synthesis and, reviewing the paper *post hoc* as they wrote the synthesis, helped to identify potential gaps which the capstone paper neatly filled. The capstone paper can also be a useful way of showing the culmination of your thinking and indications for any innovations which may occur in the future.

There are three key advantages of writing a capstone article in parallel with the synthesis:

- It helps build your confidence that the work explored in your synthesis is actually coherent.
- That the act of writing the capstone paper is good preparation for the viva – there is a requirement that the synthesis has to be written to satisfy the Board of Examiners and the published work has already satisfied academic journal reviewers. The capstone article makes you think more deeply about your work and the issues you have been writing about and, if you remind yourself of these issues and practise exploring them, then it can make the viva feel more manageable.
- At the end of the synthesis and at the end of the capstone article, you clearly identify future work streams and this has the effect of 'revving you up' in terms of momentum for the time post-viva when you may start to be able to build on these identified areas for development and exploration.

  Once you have your full number of submitted papers/artefacts for submission, together with the capstone paper (if appropriate) and a nearly completed synthesis, it is worth spending some time thinking about spin-off publications which may come from this body of work. If you have avoided writing book chapters because your PhD regulations did not allow them, now might be the time to try. Can you write a follow-up publication based on one of your papers – is it calling out for more depth, or currency, or updating? (See Insider Perspective 3.6.)

Insider Perspective 3.6 Follow-up publications

I had to write peer-reviewed articles for my planned PhD. Book chapters weren't allowed and I also wrote a capstone paper about social professionalization in health care. I felt worn out by the end of the process but, as I was finishing my synthesis and identifying future strands of work, I started to see how some of the ideas in my papers could be updated in some detail in the light of current knowledge which had emerged since I started my PhD over five years before. I identified these in my synthesis. Once I handed in my synthesis and before my viva I used this period of calm to network with colleagues and attend events. This currency helped me talk about my older work at my viva and gave me ideas for new publications which extended and modernized my work. I am actually also going to write a book chapter for a professional colleague who has been asked to write a text book for health care managers and I am taking this new opportunity.

Christian, Academic, mid-career, completed PhD by published work (prospective route), UK

4 Writing Your Synthesis

The synthesis is the key theoretical piece which illuminates the originality of your thinking, explores your 'golden thread' of connectivity and demonstrates how your work has made a contribution to the overall body of work at each stage in its development. It demonstrates the extended commitment to your studies, summarizes all your published work and distinguishes PhD by published work awards from traditional routes, as universities have different requirements and guidance for the synthesis submission, presentation and content. This chapter outlines the key expectations for the synthesis, recognizing that different universities may have slightly different regulations about content, length and the proportions of the required sections. This chapter will also specifically address how to use the synthesis to strengthen the coherence of your theme, its originality and its contribution to knowledge.

To a certain extent, making a good job of the synthesis prepares you for the viva. It is pretty much a certainty that you will be asked about the originality of your work, its coherence, how you generated your 'golden thread', and your contribution to knowledge. The examiners will be assessing whether you can show deep reflection on each of these areas. If you can manage to accomplish this deep reflection as you write your synthesis, then this will support the preparation you will need to do for your viva.

This chapter will also address how to make a start on writing and structuring your synthesis, and ways to find your coherent theme. For the purpose of this chapter, the coherent theme is referred to as the 'golden thread' – the nub of the thinking that weaves through your work and which you must make sure you elucidate in your synthesis. It will address how to identify your own originality and separate it from your co-authors' work, and also deal with the thorny issues of how much your scholarship has contributed to the knowledge in your area. There is also a discussion about the different approaches to demonstrate the impact of your work together with some practical frameworks and ideas on how to structure your synthesis. The chapter includes practical advice and the ideas from the surveys, focus groups and personal 'insider perspectives'. There are several different examples of how individual candidates came up with themes at the beginning of a prospective route, or found a theme as part of the collation of their retrospective work.

Many researchers and PhD students find the structuring element of writing articles for publication relatively straightforward and this skill develops as their career progresses. However, sometimes (according to the respondents of my survey), the structuring of the PhD synthesis can prove perplexing, especially if they feel their 'golden thread' needs strengthening. The questions they usually ask are, 'How can I get all my thoughts and ideas of many years into 10,000 words? What goes first? What should I include? How do I encapsulate all this originality into a summary?' I shall try and address these questions in this chapter.

As we read in Chapter 1, the synthesis can be called the 'doctoral statement', the 'cover story', 'the summary of work', 'the reflective piece' but, in essence, this is the key theoretical piece which illuminates the originality of your thinking, showcases and demonstrates your 'golden thread' of connectivity, and demonstrates how your work has made a contribution to the overall body of work at each stage in its development. Candidates are being asked to state the intellectual position to which their collated publications lay claim and to defend that position by argument (UKCGE, 2004). Amidst all this angst about your synthesis remember one thing: for the subject or discipline, the research carried out by you is vitally important. Many doctoral students will become the professors of the future, and most doctoral research gives rise to new knowledge, new interpretations and new explanations. The work you have published that you collate and discuss in your synthesis is your opportunity to showcase your work, your thinking, and your research plans for the future.

▶ Starting to structure your synthesis

Structuring a conventional PhD thesis – and, indeed, the synthesis for a PhD by published work – can often be more of a challenge than the undertaking of the research itself and the writing of the papers (Carter, 2009). Many candidates said to me that writing their synthesis seemed to be completely different from anything they had written before. One colleague describes her experience in Insider Perspective 4.1.

There is no hard-and-fast rule, no 'one-size-fits-all' for a synthesis – but, hopefully, the content that follows will give you ideas on how you could make a start on writing and structuring your own.

Insider Perspective 4.1   Starting your synthesis

I just didn't really know best how to start it. I knew I had to reflect, show how key ideas linked together, indicate the research journey and contextualize the stages of the research and what I'd found ... but I didn't really know how to structure it and strengthen the coherence. Should I weave in elements of reflection throughout, show at every stage what was original or just lob in the reflection at the end? In the end, I took a chronological journey looking at each emergent theme at every stage and giving them each a separate section with a reflective summary and indicators of originality woven into each section. It worked best that way and made it easier to read. I had a few false starts though.

Academic, mid-career, completed PhD by published work (retrospective route), UK

Developing a sound structure

The result of a sound structure is more than a sum of the parts; showing authorial control over structure can give a real strength and authority to prose. Your writing can covertly and overtly show your values and your self-awareness as the author. It is essential that, if you want to present your 'golden thread', and show off the originality and your individual knowledge in the best possible way, then you should give some thought to your synthesis structure. You should focus specifically on the ordering of the material, the emphasis achieved through the size of each section, and how you link up sections or use figures to allow the different themes and sections to cohere.

Writing an academic paper for publication can feel structurally constraining. You are not only writing to the structure demanded by the journal, but you also need to be aware of the customs of your academic discipline too. Research findings presented in the papers (particularly the quantitative ones) may have their own prescribed order and all will be driven by methodological considerations. In contrast to this, the structure of the synthesis itself does give you an opportunity to demonstrate the coherence, originality, passion and knowledge in the way you choose to best suit you and your writing style.

Writing your synthesis for your audience

The readers of the synthesis will be the examiners themselves; they will have to be satisfied that it meets the standards for such work and then sign off that regulatory requirements have been met. These examiners are the first audience of your synthesis, so, let your synthesis speak to them, and make sure you show how original, reflective and insightful you have been. Bear in mind there may be some regulatory requirements for the synthesis and these will differ from country to country and in different institutions within countries. For a synthesis for a PhD by published work, these usually amount to exploring and evidencing the crux of a successful PhD – originality, knowledge contribution, coherence and a reflective journey. It would, of course, be foolhardy and unnecessarily risky to ignore the basic checklist of requirements for the synthesis; however, how you knit these elements together, and your style and approach, is largely up to you.

The shift from what you need to say to what you think your reader wants to hear and understand can be tricky. This can be difficult, particularly with a PhD by published work, where you may have been immersed in a certain style of writing and absorbed by the details of the subject area at quite a microscopic level for years. If you can step outside the granular detail of your papers and try to see the content of your synthesis from the readers' perspectives, it will make your work accessible to a wider range of people and also help the examiners (some of whom will not have a detailed knowledge of the specifics of the spectrum of your career work) understand its meaning. Try to make the connections, ideas, research journey and key findings as logical, explicit and jargon-free as possible in order to involve and engage the reader.

For the traditional PhD route, handbooks on doctoral theses offer a range of structural models which, to some, can seem rather reductive and constraining. These typically focus on (for scientifically-based theses) an introduction, a critical literature review, methodology, findings, critical analysis and evaluation, and a conclusion and recommendations. Indeed, when you wrote up your research work for publication, the journal may well have requested a similar sort of structure for your paper. Kamler and Thomson (2006) feel this model does not allow the foregrounding of the argument but merely highlights the facts and process, and constrains the writer. They would prefer the values and the argument to provide the overarching structure. In the synthesis, because you are not laying out the findings of your research (these are in the individual published works), you can let the themes do just that and they can provide the framework for the structure. For a PhD by published work, Carter *et al.* (2012) state pragmatically, as they talk about theses, 'It need not aspire to being a work of art, yet it does need to convince examiners that it is an adequate example of the genre.' You may, of course, set your sights even higher and aspire to your synthesis becoming a work of art!

Considering your discipline

I mentioned earlier about being aware of the expectations and traditions of your academic discipline and how that may (or may not) influence your writing style and approach. Interestingly, if you have done a good deal of team research and have co-authored papers that you are counting in your submission, you should include consideration of this in your synthesis – it can provide fertile ground for reflection. The Bologna Process (Department for Education and Skills, 2007) emphasized the benefits of interdisciplinary research and encouraged universities as the organizations to foster this nationally and internationally. More interdisciplinary research leads to more interdisciplinary, multi-authored papers, which can result in more radical, novel ideas. However, this also leads to more co-authoring and, possibly, more tensions between the accepted publication styles and approaches for the final research output papers.

If you use any of your jointly written articles as part of your submitted portfolio of published work, you will need to address their contribution and originality as part of your synthesis. In addition, you may find that addressing tensions between co-authors' discipline conventions, how the academic work was eventually structured, processed and presented and your individual stance on the findings can actually be discussed productively as part of the reflective element of your synthesis.

▶ Reflecting on your work as part of the development of your synthesis

Using reflective theory to guide your reflective thinking process and writing

If you are discussing your own research journey and development in your synthesis, it is inadequate to offer a superficial description. It is also not enough to write, 'I reflected on the ideas that came out of Paper 1 and they were ...' You should aim to use a model of reflective theory and use it to structure your reflective writing. This will make your arguments more reasoned, organized and sequential in their exposition. One of my survey respondents (a professor and experienced examiner of PhD by published work submissions) suggests moving beyond just the Kolbian-style reflective cycle (Kolb, 1984) 'which can generate a lot of descriptive rather than analytical material'. Reflection needs to move beyond the individual level to include a critical perspective on wider issues, generalizable to beyond just that of the individual. For example, when writing my own work on health research, I used Ghaye's model (2005), which aids reflection on issues of power and inequality, and Dyke's work (2006) on contextualizing the social world. These models were valuable in helping me reflect more fruitfully on the wider applicability of my research and its coherence. The value of using these 'macro' models underpinned a more robust, holistic, critical approach to the reflective process.

An example of this is a colleague who was collating her published work on notions of power in community health settings for a retrospective published work route. She used her ability to reflect critically to help draw together an underpinning framework, acknowledging the underlying theoretical contribution from critical theory which sought to makes systems and structures of power visible. In particular, she referred to the work of Barnett (1997) and Fook (2002). Barnett's work brings together three domains of critical practice, these being critical analysis, critical reflexivity and critical action. Fook's work (p. 41) refers to the potential of critical reflection for 'emancipatory practices'. Using the application of these critically reflective theories, she strengthened the usefulness and holistic, macro-perspective of her work. She also used active, reflective writing in her research papers and in her synthesis to reflect on her professional development and the future impact of her work.

Reflective practice and using reflective writing is considered by many professions to be beneficial for professional development and an indispensable element of professional education that leads to the melding of theory and practice (Clegg *et al.*, 2002; Moon, 1999). Her submitted synthesis included a section about how theoretical models of reflection can also be used in curricula for future health students to help them understand how micro-health problems can, if analysed more critically (using the critically reflective theories of Tate (2004) or Fook (2002)), be viewed through a variety of lenses in order to promote wider discussion of the broader health issues with students. This PhD candidate was therefore in a good position to demonstrate joined-up thinking and thus enhance the coherence of her research work and research journey. It was clear that the value of using the theoretical frameworks to enhance her reflective thinking explicitly in the synthesis strengthened this process.

In the focus group, one participant who had successfully completed his PhD described an interesting approach to 'kick-starting' his thinking. He was struggling to reflect on the big macro issues of his work and whether they were significant, original and sufficiently important to write about. He also wanted to stimulate his 'passion for the area' and understand 'from the heart' why the issues he had selected were worth researching. He had identified a broad theme – in his case 'education as empowerment' – and then asked himself the following questions: 'Why am I interested in this?', 'How do I stand as an individual person subjectively in relation to different approaches to education', 'How can educational empowerment be demonstrated in these areas where my research has taken place (schools, overseas universities, different cultural communities)?', 'Why do I get cross when people do not use education to empower their students/clients?' In searching to answer these questions, he was encouraged to reflect on some of the theorists who might provide a wider, theoretical framework for developing his emergent ideas (for example, Freire (1968) and his consummate thinking about empowerment issues).

Using the chronology of research: mapping your journey

Initially, it can be difficult to make a start on writing your synthesis – putting down the first word of the draft for the structure. If you are stuck, use the simple natural chronology to enhance your reflective thinking in the first instance. Use a straightforward, earliest-to-most-recent ordering of your published work, particularly if you want to analyse your thinking on the progression of a subject or theme over time. Use the timeline as your linking motif, record when the writing and research findings actually occurred, and what changes in your thinking and research journey were generated as a result. This is a simple and effective approach. You can use flip charts and coloured pens to represent different themes to jot ideas onto the timeline or post-it notes. Some supervisors ask their students to create a physical layout of hard copies of all the papers and artefacts on a long table. They then ask probing questions about the content and findings for each of the wider portfolio outputs in the public domain that you are considering submitting. Those that are weaker and do not adhere to the strong theme are then discarded from the submission and synthesis.

Sometimes, identifying one strong coherent theme can prove difficult for retrospective candidates who have written prolifically and widely over many years. Resolving this is really a matter of co-analysis and discussion. Specific recognition and identification of the papers and artefacts that are the most original, and that have made the greatest contribution to and impact on your subject area is essential, if you are to use the most suitable coherent work in your submission and synthesis. An alternative, more focused approach for candidates on a retrospective route (particularly if you wish to analyse the growth, development and progress of your research to explore its coherence) is to look at each of your individual papers and artefacts and recollect why you wrote it; and then ask yourself:

- What were the catalysts and triggers for the research?
- What were the real challenges and breakthroughs?
- What did each reviewer say in their feedback about the paper?
- How did you act on it?
- Then ask yourself whether those comments influenced your future work and subsequent papers.

You can then map this onto a timeline to create a chart of your journey; this will provide a visual representation that could form a draft structure for your emergent synthesis.

Using mapping frameworks to help develop your synthesis

Once you have decided on the papers you are going to use in your synthesis and you have worked out the key theme(s) in your research that you are going to explore, you might find it useful to use the information in the boxes to enhance the coherence, structure, balance and navigability of your synthesis. This will also have the added bonus of making the work of your supervisor and examiner much easier. They will not have to dig about looking for evidence of your coherent themes, as it is all visually documented.

It is likely that you have more than one theme emerging from the papers you wish to submit for the award. However, once identified they may well form a more holistic coherent body of work. For example, my work focused on separate papers which explored thematic issues about team work, work in interdisciplinary settings and curricular change. However, they were all linked to health environments and used similar methodologies. It was therefore possible to show coherence through the ways team working and interprofessional learning were linked into each of my papers. It is the key idea emanating from the coherence of the themes that is the identifiable golden thread in your research and it is essential to be able to identify this. (See Box 4.1.)

You can amend this mapping as you write your synthesis, tweaking it as you go along before finalizing it. It is a useful way to show how your chosen themes (as the elements of the 'golden thread') are woven through the structure of the synthesis chapters and evidenced in different sections. An examiner can then easily see where the theme is cross-referenced in the relevant section of the synthesis and refer to this template if he or she wishes to ask you about a particular theme and how you have evidenced it in a specific section.

You can use some of the information generated from the activity in the Box 4.1 in the body of the synthesis text. For example, at the end of each section of the synthesis you may wish to write a brief, retrospective critical reflection on your stage of thinking at the time and how it related to more macro-perspectives. This is a useful tactic to employ and reading the summaries before the viva can be a good aide memoire. However, you need to bear in mind that, if you are using this technique, you may be asked about the effect of subjective retrospective analysis on bias and the truth of your research (see Chapter 6).

Box 4.1 Focusing on your key publications

This can be a useful exercise if you have a wide, diffuse portfolio of publications written over many years and want to slim them down for a more focused submission.

List your key themes from *all* the papers you wish to include in your synthesis.

- Number all the papers you want to submit for the award in chronological order.
- Note which theme is addressed in each identified numbered paper and how you have explored it.
- Have you found a paper in which your chosen themes are not well-represented? If so, you may wish to remove it from your submission.
- Note the originality of each piece of work at the time.
- Note whether each paper had any wider impact related to your identified themes.
- Then, from your chosen papers, you may wish to indicate how one theme led to another: note whether it was a change in the emergent literature, the wider policy or research context, your own workplace and so on.
- Again, consider whether any of your papers (which may be interesting either in their own right or as standalone pieces) do not show strong coherence, originality, or impact linked to your overall themes. Consider whether they should be included in your submission.

This activity can also form the basis of a figure or a table for your synthesis. It will draw examiners' eyes and will help you demonstrate the thematic coherence and impact of your work.

Still struggling with developing the coherence and structure?

The following pieces of advice might help you enhance the structure and coherence of your synthesis, if you are still stuck.

Just the headings: In discussion with a supervisor who had worked with many students on honing their synthesis of their work for the award of PhD by publication, she addressed how to enhance what she calls the 'narrative of cohesion'. She says, 'I am a great believer in topic sentences to help with cohesion. I suggest to the students that they cut and paste their topic sentences, chapter headings and all sub-headings into a blank document in order and read just the headings to see if it clearly *tells a story'*.

Dividing up the literature: Another supervisor suggested a way to support a student who is unable to manage their literature usefully. They may be overwhelmed by all the literature they have used over the years in their published work and be indecisive about what to concentrate on for the purpose of the synthesis. She suggested, 'I find it helpful to get the students to divide the literature into *background* and *polemic*: the former doesn't have to be exhaustive; in the latter, concentrate on that literature which you will hold up against your own research in the Discussion Sections where you are exploring the research journey or your contribution to knowledge.' Polemic literature will be more contentious and set out to establish one truth through a series of proofs or reasoned arguments. The background literature can then be usefully summarized, if you are analysing the contextual broad drivers to your overall body of research and the more 'polemic' literature can stimulate the triggers, critical thinking and emergent arguments which may, in turn, then have catalysed something original or alternative, or a new line of activity.

Mind mapping/spider diagrams: Tony Buzan (1974) was the early populariser of mind mapping to stimulate the generation of ideas through images and visual connections. According to Buzan, orthodox forms of note-taking do not stick in the memory because they use only the left side of the brain, leaving our creative right brain dormant. Spider diagrams and 'cognitive cartography' are based on these ideas and, while there appears to be good scientific evidence to show that images can enhance recall, it is quite clear that mind mapping may not be helpful for those with a more factual, logical and words-based learning style. There is a great variety in how and why spider diagrams and 'cognitive cartography' are used and how they are produced (Beel *et al.*, 2009).

How would you use mind mapping or spider diagrams in this context? On a practical note, I have found simple, free-form spider diagrams helpful for each paper (and, indeed, as an overview for the whole synthesis as an aide memoire prior to the viva). They can help to distil topics onto a single, memorable page through their use of colour and spatial organization (Cooke, 2013). Put the main 'golden thread' as a picture in the middle and then have a radiating branch for each idea, application, theory or sub-theme relating to it. Drawing the links between ideas and grouping ideas (including pictures) acts as memory triggers.

Choose a different colour for each publication, if you wish to draw out the key content of each paper. Also, use two additional colours indicating possible new ideas and future work from this paper, and possible connections to other papers (which you may have missed). I have used this as a tool to encourage free-thinking with others undertaking their PhD by published work generating theme links and 'golden threads'. Once complete, the diagram can be turned into linear notes to help the structuring phase, numbering the emergent ideas and then the sub-ideas in order to formulate a synthesis plan and a more solid structure. They can also be a useful tool for creating a summary overview before the viva and helping you remember it – I did one for the whole synthesis.

Triangulating your theme: Triangulation facilitates the trustworthiness of qualitative data, and the validation and reliability of quantitative data, through cross-verification from more than two sources. By examining our 'golden thread' from more than one standpoint, we can map out and explain more fully whether it is strong and consistent in a variety of environments and applications. Triangulation is not only about validation, but is also about deepening your understanding of your research. It can be used to produce innovation in conceptual framing and can lead to multi-perspective meta-interpretations (Cohen and Manion, 2000). For example, if you have used more than one method in your career research and have used different ways of asking the same question, see whether any similarities have emerged. If so, check whether this is carried forward into subsequent results in later projects. If a large number of differences have emerged from using multiple methods to ask the same question, try to seek explanations for this. This is an approach used commonly as part of action research – where contribution to knowledge can be assessed by the unique information emerging from a cycle of vigorous attempts to confirm or disprove them by questioning and referring to the literature (Dick, 1997). Triangulating your theme can help with coherence and structure. You may well perceive you have a good theme/'golden thread' but are wondering whether it is sufficiently robust, and whether you can demonstrate its value, strength and applicability in all its forms. Try asking yourself the following to triangulate your work:

> For my 'golden thread', can I apply my theory to practice? Can I demonstrate how it stems from the literature and can be explored in different areas/contexts and illuminated by my work? Can I use plainer language and reduce jargon to ensure that other readers from other subject disciplines can understand its meaning?
>
> Could my work and its theme be contextualized to different environments, subject and practice areas? If so, which? Do my newer ideas reflect ideas in an older, more established field? Is my micro-work applicable to a more macro (general) model? Are there international/local parallels? Is the work applicable globally? Is the global work actually applicable locally?

▶ Ideas for structuring your synthesis

Your individuality versus the regulatory guidance

Naturally, the structure of the synthesis will vary for each person (see Box 4.2). Your synthesis is not a research paper being submitted to a predetermined set of criteria but, rather, the means by which you present your originality; demonstrate your research journey; and voice your discipline's discourse, your reflection and your contribution to knowledge. That said, only the foolhardy would ignore some synthesis sections which may be mandatory in the regulations of the university at which you are enrolled. Looking at other syntheses available by means of your university library can be helpful, as exploring how other authors have structured their syntheses can help you establish visualizing your own. These may well be the best drivers of the decisions you make about your synthesis structure.

One person I interviewed had written many papers on assessment techniques in higher education and who thought, at first, that their 'golden thread' was about how different assessment methods empower learning in universities. She initially planned the synthesis with each chapter exploring a different assessment method, how it was reflected in each of her publications, how her view of each different method was original and how each paper contributed to the state of knowledge. This was not necessarily wrong.

Box 4.2 Questions to ask when planning the structure of your synthesis

- Looking at the contents pages, which structures in others' syntheses are most successful and easy to navigate?
- Does the structure reflect the author's research priorities and theme?
- What is practical for you? Are the synthesis chapters of similar lengths and, if not, what do the different lengths show you?
- Do headings make use of metaphor, or clear points and topics? What suits your research and synthesis theme best?
- Ask yourself what style of structure fits best with your purpose of your synthesis.
- Consider what matters most about your synthesis. Consider the deepest level of your research and the values that have influenced you.

However, on discussion with her supervisor, it was felt that what she had really been writing about over time was how the choice of assessments reflected more macro level changes in the nature and history of learning in higher education. (See Insider Perspectives 4.2 and 4.3.) A restructuring of the draft followed with a more chronological approach to the different historical changes which had occurred in the institution over time. The candidate

---

Insider Perspective 4.2 Finding the 'golden thread': PhD by existing published work

It initially struck me that my 'golden thread' was on qualitative methodology and how it illuminated the dynamics of team working. I initially structured a draft synthesis taking a different angle to qualitative methodology in each chapter. However, after reviewing my papers and selecting a slightly different combination, it was clear that the main theme was about critical reflection and how different models could be used to reflect on methodologies, team work, educational and curricular development. The key value, and the most important purpose of the research, had been to show how to enhance critical reflection in different forms and so I redrafted the synthesis to show how critical reflection underpinned each area, running it through separate sections on curricular development and methodologies. I wove in the contribution to knowledge and the originality of each theme at the end of each chapter in a sub-heading and that worked well.

Sue Smith, Author, mid-career, completed PhD by published work (retrospective route), UK

Insider Perspective 4.3 Planning to write around a coherent theme

'I think it is easier to do the route prospectively – it would be hard to look back on your work and find a focused theme and gather a series of disparate strands together.' She described how her 'golden thread' is identified as part of the main research question based on her own interest and curiosity, and fed logically through all the subsequent research objectives which are considered in the separate publications. She says, 'the programme of research and its subsequent papers are what provide the basis for demonstrating a coherent theme in the reflective account and ensure the presentation of a reasoned and rational body of work.'

Lauren, Academic, mid-career, undertaking a PhD by published work (prospective route), UK, nearing the end of the five-year registration period and preparing for her viva

explored how the different pieces of work and research on assessment and its meaning underpinned these changes. The coherence was enhanced by analysis of the emergent literature at the time and how the findings were influenced at each change by macro-level national higher education policy in the UK and in the international context.

You need to ask yourself whether your different sections are going to be based on chronology, each theme/topic, chapters on originality, knowledge and so on. How do you wish to present it? Are you going to have a reflective paragraph at the end of each chapter which might generate links forward, backwards and across themes? How might subheadings in your different sections make the links more explicit in your synthesis and tie the chapters/sections together?

What is your 'golden thread'? Think about how your 'golden thread' can be best illuminated through the structure you might choose. What are the deep values and the purpose of your research, and what do you wish to highlight? Highlighting topics /themes and supporting them by points can create a more coherent perception for the reader than an approach which takes separate points supported by topics/themes, as addressed by Davis and McKay's (1996) different structural models for writing.

▶ Coherence, originality and contribution to knowledge: the triple whammy

Coherence, originality and contribution to knowledge are the three elements essential to a high-quality synthesis. If you can show your work is coherent, has not been done this way before and that it has added something to the field, then you will have cracked it.

Ask yourself:

- Does my synthesis show that all my submitted publications are linked and that there is a clear 'golden thread'?
- Does my synthesis explain that I have done something that has not been done before?
- Does the synthesis explain what I have contributed to the body of knowledge in my research area?

If the answer to any of these points is 'no', then strengthen that element in your synthesis.

▶ The nature of 'coherence'

Central to a PhD by published work is the notion of 'connectedness' – how the content of the synthesis, the 'golden thread' and the structure all need to hang together and make the research publications and their supporting synthesis coherent. Grant (2011) usefully develops the idea of the 'logic of connectivity', describing it as a demonstration of how reasoned thought links, joins and relates all the different elements of the synthesis. She uses 'connectedness' or 'connectivity' to represent 'coherence' in her model, which we will address later in this chapter.

Articulating the connectivity

Be clear about your own method of connectedness. Make sure you are explicit within your synthesis about *how* exactly you logically linked up the ideas in your work and found your theme or your 'golden thread'? Explain the actual process you adopted in your synthesis. I analysed a range of different syntheses from successful PhD by publication candidates to explore how they articulated their connectivity and strengthened their key theme and 'golden thread'.

- *Approach 1*: Some used the 'golden thread' of one underpinning theory from their research and extrapolated it to different subject areas or environments (see Triangulation: p. 91).
- *Approach 2*: Some explored how a specific type of methodology had been used in all their papers and the methodology itself became the 'golden thread'.
- *Approach 3*: Some successful syntheses explored how their work was influenced by emergent contextual literature and policies, and how the relative framework they applied to the new literature became their 'golden thread' and brought about changes in the direction of their own work.
- *Approach 4*: Others (usually in covert or overt observational or qualitative interviewing) used meta-inference (exploring their personal stance in response to their own research questions, especially around issues of self, bias and reliability) to enhance the synergy of their publications.

There are no rules. You could use just one approach, or all of them successively, but you do need to articulate the process you use in your synthesis and make sure the same process considers *all* your publications to a greater or lesser extent.

Box 4.3   Synthesis connectivity (based on Grant, 2011)

Stage 1: Using retrospective research questions to enhance connectivity

↓

Stage 2: Using the literature in your published work to enhance connectivity

↓

Stage 3: Using underpinning theoretical work to enhance connectivity

↓

Stage 4: Using your methodologies to enhance connectivity

↓

Stage 5: Using meta-inference and new insights to enhance connectivity

---

Grant (2011) adopted a five-stage process (see Box 4.3) which used all the approaches in sequence to address, underpin and strengthen the coherence of her research and elucidate her 'golden thread'. I shall now explore some of her stages and cite examples of individuals who have used some of these approaches themselves and explored them in their own syntheses.

Using retrospective research questions to enhance connectivity
Grant (2011) refers to the theoretical work on methodology throughout her articulation. So, for her first level of connectivity, which she calls 'The Retrospective Use of Research Questions and Clustering', she examines all her eight retrospective publications and outputs. She calls them 'chronicles' to reflect the longitudinal nature of the work. She has a clear subject focus for all her papers: they examine issues relating to teacher leadership in South Africa. She has three research questions relating to her main theme and clusters the chronicles to best answer the research questions. Her third question aims to develop a theoretical side to understanding teacher leadership.

Her questions were:

- How is teacher leadership understood and practised by educators in mainstream South African schools?

- What are the characteristics of contexts that either support or hinder the take-up of teacher leadership?
- How can we theorize teacher leadership within a distributed leadership framing?

It is clear that a candidate could not, would not and should not succeed at PhD level (as it is a standard criterion for the PhD) without including a clear theoretical underpinning *but* it can be strengthened (an enhanced connectivity) in this retrospective PhD by published work route by articulating it in the synthesis about each of the published outputs (see Insider Perspective 4.4).

If you are a prospective route candidate, you ask these questions at the beginning of your research journey and review the questions linked to your papers (grouping the chronicles to them) just prior to starting your synthesis writing (see Insider Perspective 4.5).

Insider Perspective 4.4 Asking questions of research work to help plan the synthesis

For my PhD, which included a series of papers from studies which focused on an aim to explore team working and collaborative working in a range of health and higher education settings using ethnographic and other qualitative approaches, I generated a series of three research questions which I wished to answer. I wanted to include those answers and insights in my synthesis.

The questions I asked myself retrospectively about my work to inform the generation of my synthesis were:

Question 1: What were the characteristics of successful team working in multidisciplinary health settings?

Question 2: How, knowing this, can we then best teach these skills and characteristics in an interprofessional health education programme for students in Higher Education?

Question 3: What theories are evident and can be expanded from the stand alone papers which can be applied to teaching interprofessional skills in the higher education sector?

I could cluster some or all of my papers (chronicles) around each research question

This led to me being able to use Wenger's (1998) work on communities of practice and Fook's (2004) work on critical reflection to extract insights into generating an original programme for interprofessional working in higher education.

Susan Smith, Author, mid-career, completed PhD by published work (retrospective route), UK

Insider Perspective 4.5 Using research questions for planning the work and the subsequent synthesis (prospective route)

This student undertook the PhD by published work through the prospective route in Australia. Here, he describes how planning the research and devising the overall aims and questions helped the structure of the emergent synthesis.

> My initial planning process involved stating a clear overall research question which became, in the end (with a few minor tweaks), the title of my final synthesis. Each sub-research question or objective actually became a published strand which allowed me to answer the question. I then linked the originality and contribution to knowledge which I explored in the synthesis to each of these research questions in separate short chapters. This held it all together and really the 'golden thread' was the original main research questions and the findings that emerged from that. By the end, I had prepared 11 papers to submission level for my PhD by published work, 10 were published but I only submitted seven of them for the synthesis to keep it really focused. I explained the whole planning process and discussed the formation of the research questions in my synthesis at the end in a self-contained separate section. The content of this section explained how each of my papers answered all or some of the questions but that the whole was greater than the sum of the parts and added depth to the previously unexplored area.

Imran, mid-career (prospective route), Australia

Using the literature in your publications to enhance connectivity

As you start to write your synthesis, you may wish to examine each of your standalone artefacts and papers. What literature did you use to inform their writing at the time? How can you now look at the literature in each of your standalone articles in a new light? Can you expand the sections in each published article (which might have been constrained by the journal word count guidance) and explore them further to form a meatier, more synthesized review which takes into account current developments in the work, new writing and a changing external context? For example, my early PhD papers encompassed ideas about collaboration and team working, and used the core available literature at the time to inform the writing of the papers. Wenger's (2002) key work on communities of practice came later than my early papers but its substance added a new lens with which to review some of my earlier ideas. I articulated this thinking about the influence of his work in the synthesis as I worked on exploring and highlighting the connecting themes in my own work.

One of my colleagues described how she wrote extensively over a long period of time in the area of corporate social responsibility (CSR) and used the (relatively scant) literature available at the time to formulate new ideas for research questions specifically in that subject area. As new work emerged and the body of knowledge in that area strengthened, she started exploring how the new literature could be applied to different organizational cultures – that is, different business areas, charities and corporate areas. As she wrote up her synthesis, she reviewed the early scant work on CSR in the light of new models described in the new literature. This 'historical, analytical retrospective' was very useful for businesses. Her work, using the emergent thinking from the literature and combined with her earlier research and publications, demonstrated how organizations could show their employees how CSR had become a growth area and was significant as part of their company ethos. This work led on to consultancy and further research into different models that could be applied inclusively across the sector.

Using underpinning theoretical work to enhance connectivity

Is there a way that you can look at the theoretical framing underpinning all your papers and outputs to enhance the sense and reality of the connectedness? Trafford and Leshem (2002a) have emphasized the significance of articulating the importance of your conceptual framework clearly in your synthesis. This allows you to generalize your research to other areas, other models and other populations, if appropriate. You need to include details of the conceptual underpinning of your research in your synthesis and explicitly state the theoretical background to your research. How has this acted as scaffolding for your research process? Who are your key theoretical influences, and what have been the key research paradigms you have used and analysed over time? How have your conceptual frameworks informed your output, findings and ongoing work? Grant (2011) also refers to this approach as a way of demonstrating connectivity strongly in her synthesis. She used distributed leadership theory as the theoretical framing for her study, looking individually at each of her papers and analysing how each output was underpinned (to a greater or lesser extent) by leadership theory. She included this thinking in her synthesis as a separate section, writing about how the underpinning theory united her work. This helped to tie up different strands in her papers.

Using your methodological and analytical approaches to enhance the connectedness

Sometimes, an analysis of the rationale for using different methodologies in your research can help you strengthen the connected feel of your synthesis. The questions listed in Box 4.4 may help you draw out some connecting strands in your work which you then might wish to add to your synthesis, if you feel it is appropriate.

Box 4.4 Using your methodological and analytical approaches to enhance the connectivity of your synthesis

- Have you used similar methodological approaches in all your work?   YES/NO

  If YES, then consider the following:

- Are the studies that underpin all your submitted papers separate studies which use the same or different methodological approaches?
- Are they all designed to a quantitative approach and, if so, how does this give you the data you need, influence the findings and offer possible solutions?
- Similarly, if all the studies are qualitative, how did this influence your research questions, your findings, and your writing journey in terms of the findings generated?
- Would analysing each of your outputs and the methodology underpinning it be useful to explore in a chapter in your synthesis to strengthen the coherence of your works?
- If you have used a mixed methods approach across all your papers, then you might want to explore retrospectively why you adopted this stance and your reasoning for this.
- Which authors have you used? Have you used the same authors' work on methodology across all your papers? If so, why? Has this meant that you have developed a particular interest or knowledge about the particular methodological approach you have chosen? Why have particular authors' methodological approaches influenced you? Do you see similar methodological patterns across all your papers?

Grant (2011), when she addresses the connectivity of her studies, discusses how the work of Sandelowski *et al.* (2006) on mixed research synthesis studies allowed her to locate her work. This approach refers to the 'mixing of methods across studies where the data are the findings of primary qualitative and quantitative studies in a designated body of empirical research' (p. 29) – that is, looking to sum up your findings in the hope that the total sum of the data collected will be richer, more meaningful and, ultimately, help you better answer your research questions.

Using meta-inference to gain insights

Meta-analysis is 'conducting research about research' in order to identify patterns and meta-inference is how you might explain these patterns (Creswell and Tashakkori, 2007). This is another way of enhancing the connectivity of your synthesis. It involves an iterative to-ing and fro-ing activity which takes the research questions you have generated to make multiple comparisons using a grounded research approach (Glaser and Strauss, 1999). This is the discovery of theory through the analysis of data as opposed to having your hypothesis first, as preconceived hypotheses result in a theory that is not grounded in the data. This is commonly used for qualitative data analysis and you might have used this approach as part of the original research analysis for the data that underpins each of your publications. However, it can be a useful supplementary activity to enhance more macro analysis of your collated work. It can work by weaving the fractured concepts into hypotheses that work together (Glaser, 1998). You can re-examine the questions generated from each submitted paper/output/artefact referred to in your synthesis, work across them (code them and categorize them, if necessary) and formulate hypotheses based on the conceptual ideas emergent from all your papers and artefacts. It is the findings from the clusters of the papers/outputs that may inform the emerging conceptual scheme or generation of your 'golden thread' (Morse, 2003: 199). This means that you can generate your own concepts that will then show links to the overall body of knowledge and demonstrate that your work is original and new, and may shed new light on your area of scholarly work.

Sometimes, this can feel subjectively as rather overly complex and laborious. This was echoed to a certain extent by one of my survey respondents who wrote: 'Very occasionally I felt quite uplifted by an emergent meta-theme and knew it was something new and original. At other times I felt the whole process seemed unnatural, boring and forced and I was trying to find themes and connectivity from a vacuum of nothing.' It would appear that the key to using meta-inference is that you need to show that the insights from all the overall analysis are greater than the individual insights shown in each of your submitted publications and artefacts.

Using the structure and language

In addition to Grant's stages (see Box 4.3), you may wish to consider explicitly how using the structure, language and style of your synthesis can enhance the coherence and connectedness of your submitted synthesis (see Ideas for Structuring your Synthesis, pp. 92–4). The structure you choose can actually enhance the 'connectedness' of your synthesis in its own right. Once you have written your chapters and achieved a good first draft, it is time to think about editing the words and structure that you have to further enhance a sense of cohesion and flow, and to bring all the parts together. As Carter *et al.* (2012) say about thesis writing, it is now the time 'for you to be smoothing the junctions, ensuring the texture and tension of the writing is consistent and tying the parts into a whole'. Enhancing the language and structure of your synthesis can improve the sense of coherence.

The style of artefacts and publications for academic arts journals can be designed cleverly to elucidate your ideas and themes. Using simple figures, photos and flow diagrams can break up text and enhance the visual nature of all types of work (not necessarily in an arts field). Some candidates use colourful mind maps, matrices and grids to explore their research ideas and own learning. This can strengthen the coherence across the chapters, ease the reader through the academic argument and strengthen the emphasis on how the different presentation of information can strengthen your key message.

▶ Highlighting the originality of your work in your synthesis

Connectivity, the contribution to knowledge and originality are 'the big ones' to address comprehensively in your route to the successful completion of a PhD by published work. All these elements are enhanced and supported by adopting a creative, systematic and reflective approach to the analysis of your work. The concept of originality must be thoroughly explored and demonstrated within your synthesis – it is, as one of the interviewed professors said, 'The nub of it and candidates have a requirement to demonstrate it in the synthesis and in the viva'.

What is originality?

'Originality' in this area can be defined as new contributions to knowledge in a particular subject area. But the concept of 'originality' – that is, offering something not offered before – can mean different things in different subject areas. It could mean:

- a demonstration or re-interpretation of an existing theory/methodology and data; *or*
- finding new ways of analysing or applying an existing body of knowledge, *or*
- proposing a new theory or model (Park, 2005); *or*
- some deductive work – for example, a new mathematical proof or new arguments.

When a thesis by a traditional PhD route is written, it needs to demonstrate the originality of that work *at the time* and candidates will be asked specific questions about it in their viva. However, for candidates undertaking a PhD by publication, the work's originality will change and needs to be demonstrated over time. You need to be able to show that *at the time of each publication* your work was original. If you can, you need to make sure you highlight this explicitly in the text of your synthesis.

How do you spot the originality in your work?

Originality will be located and identified in a variety of ways. First, each peer-reviewed paper will contain a review (or a summary review) of the literature, the current context of practice and show how your work is new and contributing to the current state of knowledge in the area. This will be assessed by the journal reviewers. If you have a focused subject area and are writing prospectively with a clearly defined, pre-identified, focused 'golden thread', you can take forward ideas generated from each research project and each concurrent paper to ensure you foreground the originality of your work at each stage in the emergent papers. One of my survey respondents undertaking this prospective route described how she planned her synthesis at the beginning and, each time she had a paper accepted or received feedback from reviewers and her supervisor, she would write notes and learning points directly into the relevant areas of the synthesis. She said she had a separate chapter on why each paper was original *at the time* and then drew these original ideas together at the end of the chapter and the conclusion of the synthesis. She said her synthesis 'grew with her'.

If you are collating a body of work *retrospectively* around an identified coherent theme with sub-themes, then your synthesis must clearly outline how each of your pieces was original at the time of publication. You may also want to write a chapter focusing on your original contribution at each stage and reflect on how the thinking underpinning each publication has developed over time. Can you clearly show progress in the development of your original ideas? Can you show the impact on the wider community through your work? Has any of your work which has been delivered at conferences been Tweeted or reTweeted by the delegates? Can you show the global impact of your work or conference presentations through analysis of its global reach (using a social media monitoring and tracking service – some are free and some require a subscription). Can you show how your contribution was new to the subject or context at that time? Have others cited you in their work and referred to any of your work. What did they think about it? How has their work influenced yours? (See Insider Perspectives 4.6, 4.7 and 4.8.)

Insider Perspective 4.6 Originality

How did you deal with bringing out the originality in your published works, in your synthesis and in your viva?

> I made sure each of the papers specifically highlighted the new knowledge generated and how it could be contextualized by the literature available at the time. In the synthesis, I specifically explored the originality of each paper and the whole collated body of work in a mini chapter. In the viva, I was asked about it and had prepared three or four key points and some critical justification, and how it might potentially impact on original and innovative ways for new practice in social care.

Jon, Academic, mid-career, completed PhD by published work (retrospective route), UK

Insider Perspective 4.7 Originality

I took the title 'Considering cultural influences of learning and teaching on the development of the supply chain management competencies for primary healthcare workers in Pacific Island countries.' And I looked at key themes as part of this, identifying what was original in relation to the existing literature. Competency mapping in supply chain management, cultural principles influencing learning and teaching, and how new approaches to developing these competencies have been trialled. The examiners were very keen on digging out the new knowledge.

Associate Professor, mid-career, completed PhD by published work (prospective route), Australia

Are you still struggling to elucidate the originality?

It can be useful to compartmentalize areas of your work in order to explore the presence and evidence of originality. Sometimes, longstanding, competent researchers who are collating their work for publication are almost too familiar with the holistic nature of their work and its overall impact to examine it in deconstructed separate chunks. This means they can fail to elucidate the originality in the synthesis in sufficient detail. If you are struggling to tease out the different components that make your work original, then try to break the work down into separate parts (such as theory, methodology, analysis, actual findings at the time). Also, do some mind mapping to see whether you are prompted to consider the originality of *each* part in *each* chosen piece of published work. You could then consider each part's originality at the point of publication and then either update it or compare it with the state of knowledge and currency of the present-day perspective.

Insider Perspective 4.8 Originality

My claims for originality related initially to two publications – effectiveness evidence about training and educational development workshops which previous literature reviews in the field had identified as significantly lacking ... In addition, some of my work which featured in another publication were deemed sufficiently original as to be picked up by the national press. [The originality] was about how students learn from each other. All the rest of my publications build on this and outline a short, simple and inexpensive intervention which can significantly improve student learning. This is what I am most proud of ... in my last publication I have produced a radical practical alternative to current practice ... which would overcome a number of existing problems ...

This all led to lots of correspondence and, subsequently, I received testimonials from leading educational developers in the UK and overseas because they cited them in workshops and presentations and in literature reviews here and in the States.

Professor, widely published internationally and within five years of retirement, completed PhD by published work (retrospective route)

The concept of originality when you are a joint author: teasing it out

This is a big question. The examiners will be interested in teasing out *your* view of originality from your submitted work. It is hard for an examiner to do this from a co-authored article where a list of co-authors makes it nigh on impossible to separate your contribution from those of others. You need to do the work for them. An examiner of the PhD by published work viva said, 'The candidate really needs to state their own originality and be prepared to defend it. This might be different from a written thesis particularly if the original papers have been in publication for a few years.' It is therefore imperative when you write your reflective piece/synthesis that you show your own contribution to the originality of the work in the content of the synthesis.

So how best can you bring out your contribution to the originality when you work with co-authors? Initially, you should submit a pro forma listing co-authors' relative contributions in each paper you are submitting for your PhD by existing published work and their relative percentage contribution. Use this table as a baseline (cross-referencing it into the body of the text of the synthesis) when you discuss your own original contribution, that of others and their work relative to your own synthesis theme, and the overall originality of the paper and your own body of work. Look at your co-authored papers. Ensure that you explore in the synthesis what your individual contribution was to each research project which underpinned the joint paper.

If you are undertaking a PhD by published work prospectively within a five-year registration time frame, it is common sense to sort out any co-authoring contributions as you go along. Explore the progression of the originality of your work through your single-authored papers specifically and make it explicit that these are your *own* ideas. Explore how your co-authored papers build on your earlier single-authored work and, in addition, the actions or new work you did individually that built on the work of your combined co-authored papers? Evidence of originality should be addressed explicitly in your synthesis, outlining how often your work has been cited and what others have written about your work. You should also describe follow-on work of your own and how you have followed through and developed your original ideas. You should aim to consider what your own original contribution offered to the overall body of knowledge now and at each stage in your publishing journey.

▶ Your contribution to the body of knowledge

In the content of the synthesis, you must justify how your research and publications as a whole made a contribution to the existing body of knowledge.

In the main, the contribution to the body of knowledge at the time is contained within the publications and needs to be summarized in the synthesis. However, the UKCGE (2004) indicates that, occasionally, some institutions might have a specific requirement for the synthesis to present a critical analysis of the significance of the publications. Some universities ask for the published work to be placed in the context of other research and critiqued, and then the matter of outlining *just* your contribution in the synthesis becomes much less straightforward. UKCGE (2004) argues that this then becomes more like a traditional award where the contribution is the critical account of the intellectual position presented by the candidate. The publications then become supporting evidence – critics of this have suggested that such a construction is unfavourable and 'necessarily somewhat *post hoc*' (UKCGE, 2004: 19).

You need to ask what *your* work has added to the thinking in your chosen area and explain this clearly to the examiners. Outlining your contribution to your subject knowledge and discipline is one of the essential elements of successfully achieving a PhD. Explore the contextual impact of your work in your subject area – have you filled a gap in existing knowledge and has this influenced practice or a change in thinking? Is it worth considering what you are already doing to show you are *actively* using your research as a contributor to the body of knowledge? Have you been asked to attend a conference to speak about your research, or are you already delivering national or international workshops and presentations around your subject area? This can be another useful indicator that you are contributing to the field; it should be detailed in your current curriculum vitae and explored in your viva, too.

Reading widely, filling gaps and applying and disseminating the findings

Reading around the subject area, identifying gaps in knowledge and undertaking research which can contribute to the filling of those gaps is a good way to begin evaluating whether you have made a contribution to the overall knowledge base. You might be able to evidence that you have at least partially proved to have plugged the gaps. You need to address this specifically in your synthesis and then perhaps map your key research findings to a time line, then justify and explain this.

Being puzzled

Sometimes 'being puzzled' is a good starting point for evaluating your research contribution (see Insider Perspective 4.9). When you start looking and enquiring beyond your own subject area, you may well notice gaps in your own knowledge. This might trigger further investigation into problem-solving and undertaking some sort of enquiry to fill the gaps and solve the perceived puzzle.

Insider Perspective 4.9 Contribution to knowledge

Another member of the group discussed a different sort of puzzlement while addressing how he could justify how his research contributed to the body of knowledge in his discipline. He had a discrete subject area which focused on globalization and internationalism. He described how, through extensive reading during his research, through conversations at conferences, he would ask himself what he was puzzled by. If there was no evident answer he would specifically use 'What am I puzzled by?' as a research question to formulate new areas for work.

He gave several examples and was able to justify how his work in specific areas had made a new contribution. He also described how, by devising his own model and using it as a key word for searching in his subsequent published work (in his case, 'cross cultural capability'), he was subsequently able to track these words in papers from authors who had subsequently cited him. He was then able to show how others had applied his ideas in different ways and, hence, was able to prove and cite the impact of his work.

Academic, three years prior to retirement, completed PhD by published work (retrospective route), UK

Making new connections and having an inquiring mind
Contributing to the body of knowledge in your subject field does not necessarily mean brand new, off the wall novelty. Some academic staff apply and integrate existing ideas into their new thinking. This application and integration, and its subsequent re-interpretation, can be just as valuable as the idea of discovery and novelty. One person felt her work was new and contributed to knowledge because it was about 'new ways of thinking about and applying a model that already existed'. She described how she explored the application of Chickering and Gamson's (1987) principles for undergraduate education in a range of different learning environments and drew new conclusions about emergent thinking and future developments from a range of papers which emerged from her initial study.

You should reflect critically on your ideas relating to aligning and applying new principles by asking yourself whether these ideas have ever been connected before. Ask yourself: Do these ideas fit together? Have others done this? Am I the first to do this? If you can answer 'yes' to these questions, then you need to explore in more depth how these ideas have contributed to the body of knowledge overall. Then, if that work and those ideas are published in the public domain, you should be able to identify in your synthesis how you have contributed to a unique body of knowledge in areas which might not have dovetailed or been considered together before. You may well also be asked to follow up on this area in your viva voce examination.

▶ Impact of your work

What impact has your work had? Who has read it? Who else has cited it? You need to make this clear in your synthesis and be prepared to explain the repercussions of your work in your viva.

How can you show your work has had impact?
Research Councils UK (RCUK) defines impact as 'the demonstrable contribution that excellent research makes to society and the economy'. Research impact embraces all the diverse ways that research-related skills benefit individuals, organizations and nations. These include:

- fostering global economic performance;
- increasing the effectiveness of public services and policy; and
- enhancing quality of life, health and creative output.

Academic impact is part of this – that is, academic advances, across and within disciplines, advances in understanding, methods, theory and application. Can you show your work has done any of this? A key aspect of this definition of research impact is that impact must be demonstrable. It is inadequate to focus on activities that simply promote research impact, such as putting on a conference or publishing a paper, however good it is. You must be able to provide evidence of the impact of your research. For example, that it has been taken up and used by policy-makers (on whatever scale – it does not have to be huge) and/or has led to enhancements in business or organizations. Above all, research must be of the highest quality: you cannot have impact without excellence.

Using citation indices, publication counts, journal impact factors or h-indices and so called 'alternative metrics' (see the next section: Bibliometrics) is another way to help identify the originality, contribution to knowledge and impact of your existing published work in the wider research and academic community. It is valuable and essential to collect data about the impact of your work. If you can show how often your papers and outputs have been cited by other authors, this can form a useful basis for a discussion in your synthesis about the dissemination of each of your papers and their value. You could also, for example, use data from academia.edu (a social networking site for academics to share research), Research Gate weekly statistics scores, testimonials, citation indices and publication sales to strengthen the impact content of your synthesis.

One colleague, who writes about finance metrics and methodologies, measured his contribution by the number of times his papers had resulted in external contacts and his being invited as a keynote speaker at an academic conference, or for external consulting work. Other colleagues who had films or recordings in the public domain cited the venue and showing figures at influential festivals and cultural events, and explained this in their syntheses. You may well be asked about the impact of your work in your viva – be prepared to explain it.

Bibliometrics for impact

'Bibliometrics' refers to the quantitative measures used to assess research output – that is, publication citation data analysis. It can be useful for a student submitting a PhD by existing published work to include evidence generated from these bibliometric tools in their final synthesis. Bibliometrics can complement the qualitative processes your work will already have undertaken as part of its peer review for journal publication (Pendlebury, 2008) and can be a useful, easily understood and transparent way to show the impact and spread of your work. Most universities will have specialist librarians or research staff who can help support you with this and your advisor/supervisor should be able to suggest someone who can help you in your particular field.

Nick Sheppard, Repository Developer at Leeds Beckett University and Technical Officer for the UK Council of Research Repositories describes the usefulness and scope of bibliometrics in Advice from Experience 4.1.

Advice from Experience 4.1 Bibliometrics

Your fundamental metrics are the number of research outputs you have produced and how often they have been cited by your peers.

Outputs may comprise peer-reviewed journal articles, papers in peer-reviewed conference proceedings, published abstracts, authored books and chapters. The relative import of each may vary according to your discipline. For example, journal articles are the gold-standard in STEM (Science, Technology, Engineering and Maths) subjects in the UK.

Citation by one's scholarly peers has long been the established measure of scientific influence and impact. In the modern information environment, citation data can be derived from third-party academic indexing services including Web of Science and Scopus, both of which require a licence to access, usually through your university library. Dissertations, books and chapters are not covered, however, and Google Scholar is a free alternative that has broader coverage but also lacks the quality control of the commercial services. It is important to note that citation data from each source may vary.

Citation patterns themselves vary considerably across disciplines so it is important to be aware of practice as it relates to your own academic area. You should also be aware of the relative impact of where and how your outputs are made available – a major international conference obviously has more prestige than a local or departmental conference and is likely to provide further reach. Similarly, the Journal Impact Factor (JIF) is a popular way of identifying the most highly cited journals in a given field and is derived from the average number of citations to articles in the journal over the preceding two years (Thomson Reuters, 1994).

Your h-index takes into account both your publication count and number of citations (Hirsch, 2005) and is derived from the number of outputs (Np) that have been cited h number of times; for example, if you have 20 outputs, 10 of which have been cited at least 10 times each, you

→

will have an h-index of 10. It measures both the productivity and the impact of the published work (usually used in science fields).

While a useful indication of impact and value, traditional bibliometrics have limitations; they are necessarily retrospective and can lack context; citation may be for negative as well as positive reasons (e.g. errors) and they can be manipulated by self-citation. The h-index is bounded by the total number of publications and really only works properly comparing scientists working in the same field. There is also debate about the validity of the impact factor, which many argue has a distorting influence on science. JIF is also arguably less important as article-level metrics become more prominent, partly as a result of scholarly communication moving increasingly online to an Open Access model (Antelman, 2004) – that is, broadly speaking, scholarly materials available online to users at no cost. So-called alternative metrics, or 'altmetrics', are increasingly important in this sphere and comprise, for example, 'how many times an article has been bookmarked, blogged about, cited in Wikipedia and so on' (Piwowar, 2013).

www.altmetric.com/ is valuable and collates a number of altmetrics. But altmetrics also have their pros and cons – they can offer a valuable insight into social activity which is inherently more timely; however, they can easily be manipulated and sharing on blogs, Twitter or Facebook does not necessarily translate directly to 'impact' though there is some evidence that they are positively correlated with citations (Costas *et al.*, 2014).

Increasingly, universities utilize software to harvest and aggregate research outputs and related citation data (including altmetrics), and may employ specialized staff that can help you describe your research impact.

If you are a member of staff at a university, or an enrolled research student, your institution may have a licence for a web crawler tool that can identify publication frequency and impact, e.g. Elements by Symplectic is one example of licensed software bought by universities to search automatically for third party data sources such as Web of Science or Scopus. Data sources like these only cover peer-reviewed papers and do not include monographs, audio outputs and book chapters, so may not always cover the whole range of the student's submitted work. You need to remember that many universities do not allow book chapters or monographs as part of their regulatory requirements for existing published work submissions.

If the data on publication frequency is useful for you, then you should include it in your synthesis and use it in your viva, if asked about the impact of your work.

▶ Finishing off your synthesis: the icing on the cake

There is a great deal of literature on how to structure traditional theses and a range of good standard PhD handbooks, if you need additional help with academic writing (Parry, 2007; or Rountree and Laing, 1996). The pointers that now follow relate specifically to how to strengthen a synthesis for a PhD by published work submission and how to elucidate the triple whammy of coherence, originality and contribution.

Using footnotes

A useful tip is to use footnotes to show connectivity between synthesis sections, and between each chapter of the synthesis and the submitted papers and artefacts. So, for example, you can have separate synthesis chapters focused on literature linkage, theoretical underpinning and specific insights emergent from the papers. Use footnotes to make cross-links *between* the chapters to show your joined-up thinking. Similarly, use them to link the content of each chapter to each paper/artefact that you have chosen to submit. This will enhance coherence. It will also provide a useful aide memoire as you prepare for your viva, where being asked about coherence is highly probable.

The contents page for the synthesis

There are three rules to follow for a contents page, I think. It needs to invite readers in, it needs to be simply structured, and it needs to show potential examiners at a glance how you have structured your work and indicate to them what you think is important. Your key views and theme(s) link together, and the relationships between the parts and the whole should be evident through the clear structuring of the contents page. Although software will build up your contents page even after you have finished writing, it is worth keeping a draft of how it is progressing and how it might shape up as a work-in-progress document. This overt plan might stop your wilder writing excesses and also prevent you wasting time and effort writing unnecessary words which may then have to be culled because you drifted too far from your pre-planned synthesis structure. Refer to the activity at the end of this chapter to help you plan your structure. Many examiners said they routinely review the contents page before the viva, regarding it as a useful signposting tool to assess the organization and outline of the work.

The title of your synthesis

The thesis title is the most obvious signpost. Good titles only ever crystallize towards the end of the PhD study so, if you are on a prospective route, do not worry if you do not have a title – just write to your planned coherent theme. It is important, though, to keep the title simple and not too local. If your work focuses around research done in just one university, then do not refer to the university in the synthesis title. Create a title for the work that references the thematic, conceptual and substantive content of your research, and keep it jargon-free and searchable. Watch out, though, some universities have regulations that make it very hard to change the thesis title once a certain point in the process has passed. Also, some universities have tight word limits – often only a 15 to 20 words maximum.

The abstract

The abstract is a high-level overall summary of the synthesis. Think of it as 'the elevator pitch for experts' (Ruger, 2013). It should summarize the context, core theme, limitations and background to your overall work, and give a realistic picture of methods, achievements and limitations. The content of the abstract you write for the top of your synthesis must include reference to your work's originality and how it has contributed to the body of knowledge. Although, in some ways it can be best to write the abstract as the very last element, an early draft is typically needed at the time when the supervisor invites potential examiners. This draft should be revisited and checked again before submitting the complete synthesis and the body of work prior to the viva. An experienced examiner commented, 'As an examiner I have learned to read the abstract another time after having finished reading the thesis: Far too often I have noted that some of the good intentions were not carried out, but are still promised in the abstract. This part of the thesis warrants particular attention to detail and style, as it will be circulated much more widely and read more often, than the whole thesis. The best abstracts I have seen summarize the thesis in the first sentence and expand on this in the remainder of the page.'

It is important not to confuse the abstract you write for your PhD by published work synthesis with the abstracts you will have written for each of your submitted peer-reviewed papers. Your synthesis abstract, by its very nature, will be less detailed, show generalizability (i.e. that the key themes can be extrapolated to other disciplines, models, practice), be more holistic and have briefly to encapsulate the 'golden thread', contribution and theoretical underpinning of all your coherent submitted work. Both synthesis and individual journal paper abstracts will have prescribed (but different) format requirements. Your university's degree regulations and guidance are likely to specify formal, abstract requirements for the synthesis submission, and its content and word limit (usually about 300 words).

The front matter

This is the part of the synthesis that appears before the body of text – that is, that comes before the introduction. It starts with a title page, the format of which will normally be prescribed by degree regulations, or can be gleaned from other theses in the library of the institution. Then, there is usually an optional page with a dedication followed by the abstract. The degree regulations are likely to require a particular declaration; for example, that this is all one's very own work and that no part of the thesis has been submitted as part of any other degree or qualification. Typically, any acknowledgements come after this.

Acknowledgements

The synthesis is a formal piece of writing and, as such, necessary constraints need to be implemented. However, in the dedication and acknowledgements you can let your character and personality shine through. However, take care that you and your colleagues, your examiners and future employers cannot be embarrassed by the content. By the time you get to the stage of writing acknowledgements for your work and synthesis, you may either feel totally exhausted, or in the most elated mood ever, and be tempted to give in to wild emotional writing. If you write in your acknowledgements that doing a PhD was the most stressful and frightening experience ever, how will future employers interpret this when the same person applies for a research post? This is not the right place to give negative feedback about the level of support that you received from your university. In particular, one should refrain from what can be seen as hidden messages to advisors, colleagues, the university or the host country.

The introduction to your synthesis

As Carter *et al.* (2012) describe, if you were having a dinner party you would not serve up the lavish dinner the instant your guests took off their coats; you would usher them into a warm house and offer them a drink before moving on to the main event. Similarly, your synthesis needs to achieve the same, and build a sense of anticipation and familiarity preparing the reader for what is to follow.

The key features of a good introduction are that it should offer a summary of the subject matter and have a sense that you are moving the reader forward. Make sure you clarify in the introduction to your synthesis a quick summary of the purpose, theme and time span of your research work. If you are writing a reflective synthesis describing your own research journey, the use of 'I' from the first paragraph is appropriate. The synthesis is not an objective exposition of research findings written passively. It is an explanation and justification of your research over time, and you will have views about how it was conducted, your findings, your themes, and your future – 'I' is entirely appropriate to personalize the passion you have for your ideas.

Literature

For a traditional PhD thesis, a comprehensive critical literature review is included which explores the state of the current knowledge in the area, the background and the gap which the research question/statement aims to answer and fill. However, for a PhD by published work, a full literature review will underpin every research project and be summarized in each output. A summary critical literature review will have been encapsulated in each peer-reviewed publication, and quality assured by the peer reviewers and the journal in which you publish each paper. For your synthesis, you do not need to include a repeat of the literature review you undertook for each published paper. What you do need to do is summarize the key texts and papers used over time in your work noting:

- which have been the most influential in informing all your research to date over time;
- regarding research:
  - o any key gaps which your research filled at the time after you had critiqued the available literature
  - o how newer literature might have subsequently answered the questions your research posed
- any recent literature in your area of interest which has not been reviewed in your peer-reviewed publications which is encouraging you to think about developing the 'golden thread' of your research in the future.

The end bit

You need to pull the strands of your synthesis together, but *how* you do this in your synthesis is up to you – check your university's guidance on this. On reviewing a series of regulations and guidance notes from different universities, and listening to the views of candidates who have successfully completed their PhDs, some or all of the following are required when you reach the end stage of your synthesis writing:

- It is worth summarizing your theme, repeating its impact and its ramifications and applicability to other disciplines and environments.
- Cite any recommendations or conclusions your *whole body of work* might have generated.
- End on a note that looks to the future.

- Indicate whether any further work has already been taken forward by others, outline its potential in some detail, and how you might wish to take it forward.

Self-criticism in the last chapter

The last chapter in the synthesis should usually address all the overall conclusions and discussions of the presented work. One of the goals of a synthesis is to demonstrate your critical thinking, and this includes being critical of one's own work. It is considered good practice to have a subsection in the last chapter that deals with the limitations of the whole body of your presented work. This allows you to focus on the boundary of what has been achieved and creates another natural opportunity to demonstrate your own understanding of the contribution you have made. It is important to exercise critical power for a realistic assessment of one's contributions – one should not be bashful, neither should one exaggerate. Also, you should certainly use the content of this section in your synthesis as an aide memoire for your viva. Its core content and main points should be written in a way that shows you really understand your work and helps you articulate its limitations and scope to your viva examiners. As you look back on your body of work, you may feel that some individual papers/outputs mentioned in your synthesis may not have made much individual impact at the time but, combined with some of your other outputs and the benefit of the retrospective view, that they generated useful research-led insights. Consideration of this, if it is relevant for you, may be worthwhile. It may also be useful, depending on the level of critical reflection you have adopted in your synthesis, to summarize how the research work has impacted on *you*, and what you have learnt between your first and last outputs. This will almost certainly be explored in your viva voce examination.

▶ Your future work

Some of the critical analysis undertaken as part of synthesis writing will lead to thoughts about future work. Good research always opens up new questions, and a synthesis subsection about future work helps with the voicing of thoughts on this. Almost inevitably, you will have had more plans for research than you could manage.

Giving an informed view of how best to continue a particular line of enquiry will demonstrate your academic research credentials. Sometimes, the quality of research carried out shines more brightly when illuminating the path ahead rather than by falling on what has been solved. End your synthesis on a positive note. Sometimes your work, when viewed as a whole, will have led to deeper insights, or have given rise to reasoned recommendations; these should be put into the last chapter.

▶ Advice from experience: a successful synthesis

Reluctant as I am to link 'top tips' to a long-term, deeply reflective and robust research process, I am equally reluctant to omit these ideas from successful colleagues who have successfully completed synthesis writing as part of their now completed PhD. It is common sense but worth reading simply to assure yourself that you are probably following this advice anyway (see Advice from Experience 4.2).

Advice from Experience 4.2
A successful synthesis: top 10 tips

1. Keep on top of your references – use a reference manager system.
2. Signpost your reader to key themes and content throughout your synthesis introduction. This helps with the sense of cohesion – keep referring to what is to come.
3. Keep records as you work, being particularly careful to save different versions of the connective narrative so that you can step back if you need to.
4. Make sure your 'golden thread' is clear in the abstract and explicit in every single chapter of the synthesis.
5. Know what to leave out – the temptation with a long backlist of publications is to throw everything into your submission but this dilutes the coherence of the message in your synthesis.
6. If you write a capstone paper for publication (see Chapter 3), include some key points from its content and thinking in the synthesis.
7. Do not repeat yourself in your concluding chapter; try to stand back and look at the research and the projects as a whole.
8. Have a 'critical friend' read the final draft and, if they are short of time, ask them if the originality, contribution and coherence stand out and are well-explained and justified.
9. Write the abstract for the synthesis at the end of the process – include the 'golden thread', key reflection on originality, its contribution, impact and future direction in its content. Make it punchy and pithy.
10. Give sufficient time for finishing off and proof-reading – it takes longer than you expect and is not just about applying a spell-check programme!

Before you print your final copy of the synthesis for submission, answer the questions in Box 4.5. This activity may help reassure you that you have done everything in your power to present your work at its best and to the best of your ability.

Box 4.5 Final checklist for your synthesis

Have I summarized each publication submitted and the co-author percentage contributions? (Check your regulations about whether this needs to be in the synthesis or in a separate attached document).

Yes ☐   No ☐

Is there a strong coherent theme in the synthesis and do I explain this in the abstract? Do I bring out the inter-relationship between the publications and how they each illuminate the theme and contribute to it?

Yes ☐   No ☐

Does my synthesis demonstrate the originality of work?

Yes ☐   No ☐

When I read the synthesis, does it indicate how I have contributed to the current state of knowledge relating to my subject area and coherent theme?

Yes ☐   No ☐

Does my synthesis indicate how some of the ideas might be generalizable to other subject areas/communities?

Yes ☐   No ☐

Have I commented on the reception of my publications as indicated by citations and reviews, impact measures and, if appropriate, the standing of the journals in which they were published?

Yes ☐   No ☐

---

5 Working with Your Supervisor

This chapter addresses how to optimize the help available to you and, specifically, how best to work with your supervisor to achieve the greatest doctoral experience. One of the cons of doing published work routes is the sense of isolation that can be felt. Using networks and supervisors effectively can go some way to reduce this.

In theory, if you are doing a retrospective PhD by published work, you do not need a supervisor – your work has already been quality assured by your peer reviewers. However, candidates writing prospectively will have one for the whole registration period to take an overview and give guidance through the research and the writing for publication. I will take you through some of the work on the emotional experience of doing a PhD, and use examples from advisors' and students' experiences. Real-life tips relating to how to make the most of your advisor/supervisor are included at the end of the chapter.

▶ When is a supervisor not a supervisor and do you need one?

Supervisory experiences differ somewhat for retrospective PhD by published work students from those on a traditional PhD route. In the UK, when a student enrols for a traditional style PhD, they are allocated a trained supervisor or a supervisory team (QAA, 2011a) to support their research training and thesis writing-up for the duration of their studies. The international supervisory system is largely consistent with this approach. The supervisor(s) will typically work with a student who is linked to support their own research in their own specialist area and is, essentially, the quality assurer of the research undertaken.

The supervisor(s) will check the student is undertaking the research ethically, and is capable of collecting and analysing data effectively, and interpreting it critically. The supervisor on a traditional route also has a role in helping to encourage the student to see how their work links to a wider body of knowledge and supports them in the writing-up of the thesis. Their key role is to keep the student on track and facilitate the production of high-quality research work. This role is similar for a student doing a prospective PhD by published work although, specifically, in addition, the supervisor(s) will be helping the candidate write for publication (rather than a thesis) and concurrently help to map the student's research direction and coherence from the beginning of the enrolment to the submission of the synthesis. All supervisors will also support the individual in the preparation for the viva voce defence of the corpus of work.

The role of the supervisor for the PhD by existing published work route

However, for a PhD by existing published work, it is clear that a supervisor in the conventional definition of the term is not required – the role is quite different. To be picky, the terminologically is incorrect; they should not be called 'supervisors' because they are not supervising anything. Their role for students on this route is purely *advisory* – to help with the selection of the publications for submission, to advise the student about the writing of the synthesis, to support in the identification of the 'golden thread' and with the preparation for the viva. The candidate's publications will, of course, already be peer-reviewed and complete.

In the UK, the QAA Quality Code Chapter B11 on Research Degrees (2011a) refers consistently to the term 'supervisor' for all routes, and the general literature on PhD support usually refers to anyone in a key mentoring role as a 'supervisor'. Most official university documentation also reflects this terminology so, for the purpose of this chapter, the words 'advisor' and 'supervisor' will be used to mean the same thing for PhD by published work candidates, meaning the person allocated to *mentor* the candidate through the PhD process. Although the UKGCE (2004) comments on the increased prevalence of universities that now formally appoint an 'advisor' rather than a supervisor, this report also points out that, if a university (generally a minority) regards the existing published work degree as one in which publications are used to support a unifying critical statement about an intellectual position, then the appointment of a 'supervisor' might be appropriate. On the other hand, most universities clearly regard the existing published work degree as one to be awarded for the contribution to the field as made by the collated publications and summarized for the synthesis, and this would require an 'advisor' to guide the candidate.

Whatever their title in the university, their role for a retrospective published work route is clearly not the same as the supervisor for the traditional PhD route (who, as stated, has a quality assurance role in terms of how the research project for the thesis is conducted) – thus, the role term 'advisor' is closer to the mark for me. The 'supervisor/advisor' for retrospective published work students may advise their candidate on the synthesis – how to bring out the coherence, the themes and the originality. They cannot 'supervise' the research because that has already been done and written up. The peer-review process undertaken when the candidate submitted the articles to the academic journals is the measure of the student's rigour, the clarity of the writing and the quality of the research. A paper may have to go through several revisions before it is finally accepted by the journal and it is this process that mirrors the iterative process of the supervisor working with the student on a traditional PhD. A student would usually be allocated their 'advisor' on enrolment. Typically, the advisor will support them through the year's allocated time as they write up their synthesis. Their role is not to comment on the quality of the research (as noted, this has been done already through the peer-review process) but, rather, to encourage the student to be clear on the highlighting of their themes, facilitate reflection on their work in a wider research context, ask them to reflect on any future research directions they can put in their synthesis, and support them in the defending of their ideas and thinking for their viva.

For students undertaking a prospective PhD by published work, the supervisory role is more traditional – supporting the students to write the papers and undertake the research work, and keeping them on track during the required timescale. Quite often, in the last year of synthesis writing (for any publications route you are undertaking), you may well have group sessions with other students on these routes to support your synthesis writing. If you are a student on the prospective route, some supervisors will run synthesis support sessions for *all* their PhD by published work students who are approaching submission because, by that stage, the quality assurance role for the prospective route students is complete. One supervisor described how she set up tight, joint-meeting schedules for all her published work students during their synthesis writing year. These schedules included everyone's deadlines and times when other candidates were available to meet for advice and networking. At some universities (e.g. The Open University), PhD by existing published work students are allocated a mentor in the year up to registration. Once registered, they then have a more formalized allocated supervisor/advisor for the year of registration.

What is most important about this debate is that the candidate needs advice and guidance to learn about articulating the contribution to knowledge and developing the cohesion of their published work. The title is immaterial – it is the activity in the role and the relationship that is important.

The typical picture

PhD study by any route is challenging and the supervisor will be a key support in the process. With a retrospective PhD by existing published work, you will only be allocated an 'official' named supervisor when you register for your award – that is, after you have sufficient published work, and as you begin to write up your synthesis and start to reflect on the core themes in your work. It is quite usual to register when you have enough papers to meet the requirements of the award as requested by your chosen university. You will typically be allocated two supervisors by your university. You may (or may not) have some choice in this and, very often, your Director of Studies (or first supervisor) might be someone from whom you have sought advice in the past as part of your ongoing writing. Usually, PhD students on the traditional thesis-based route work with their supervisor over five years, often co-presenting at conferences, defending and justifying their methodology at research seminars and symposia, and meeting with their supervisor as they learn their research skills and how to explore and analyse the findings they may be generating.

The picture appears to be more varied with published work students. Many retrospective candidates are active, established researchers known in their field who have simply not had the opportunity to undertake a doctorate, but whose long academic career has remained active, outward-facing and whose publications are of a PhD equivalent (i.e. original, coherent, and contributing to the knowledge base in their area). Other candidates for this award may come to their advisor having had (unlike the traditional PhD student) minimal opportunity to defend their work in public.

A PhD student on the published work route may have written and submitted the papers for peer review several years before, may be writing and submitting alone and not still be part of an active research group/centre, and may not have had the opportunity to attend so many seminars and conferences to defend work recently. It is arguable that this candidate should show on application – and prior to being accepted on the award – that he or she is active and contributing to the field. If the filtering has not been successful and this appears to be the case, the supervisor/advisor needs to give the candidate opportunities for challenge and practice in articulating the themes of their work by integrating them into existing research centres, encouraging conference presentations, actively exploring issues with them, and/or providing a network of fellow students who can work together to hone their verbal defence of their work and synthesis in preparation for the viva.

▶ The supervisory experience for the student: emotions and process

Emotions and the doctoral experience

All doctoral study involves a huge number of challenges – accomplishing the writing, constructing a scholarly identity, maintaining momentum and dealing with the normal life issues which occur during your doctoral enrolment. Emotions are fundamentally implicated in all human behaviour; they shape our views, impact on our thought processes, affect our communication skills and motivate action (Lupton, 1998). Indeed, attempting to understand the 'emotionally laden' (Schutz et al., 2006) nature of learning has prompted much research into the role of research in educational settings.

Hughes and Tight (2013) relate the PhD learning and work experience from the student's and supervisor's view as a journey, comparing it with metaphors in the *Pilgrim's Progress*. They write that 'The message of travailing against all obstacles, through the strength of the inner spirit' speaks strongly to individualism and resilience (Hughes and Tight, 2013: 766), and ignores how the development of good study habits, rigour, knowledge and skills (the relevant work processes) is also an essential component for a successful PhD. The writing process and the formal registration for the synthesis writing can add up to many years; this means the stresses vary and must be dealt with over the long haul. This is recognizably wearing – job changes, publication rejections, personal changes, financial pressures, family issues, inconsistent mentoring and support, and the juggling of writing with paid work can be challenging. That said, some have felt that the fact that the work becomes embedded in 'normal life' and the ongoing thrill of publication success and the deep satisfaction on finally receiving the award at the end of the process make it all a rewarding process. Pekrun et al. (2002: 96) identify the functions of emotions as, 'Preparing and sustaining reactions to important events and states by providing motivational and physiological energy, by focussing attention and modulating thinking and by triggering action-related wishes and intentions.' How do we see these processes impacting on the doctoral experience and how can you use these emotions to your benefit?

Cotterall (2013) summarizes the range of emotions which affect the doctoral experience for better and worse, and explores how motivation ensures students stick with the process until graduation. Anxiety can curtail a PhD student's ability to write (Castello et al., 2009), but dealing with stress effectively and developing key coping strategies can enhance achievement of the intended outcomes – that is, in this case, a completed synthesis and

> **Insider Perspective 5.1   Finding a supervisor**
>
> I suppose I don't have to cope with a small grant and constrained finances as I am doing my publishing as I progress through my career with my full-time, paid job but I still have stresses – I am not going to fully enrol and find a supervisor until I am ready to publish and think about my synthesis but sometimes I think that I won't be able to even find a supervisor to suit my subject area, it is taking so long two of my key advisors have left and the rejection cycle of papers you need to complete to get your award grinds you down over a long time. Two steps forward, one step back. Sometimes I wish it was short and sharp like a traditional PhD!
>
> **Sarah, Academic, early career, working towards a PhD By published work (retrospective route), UK**

successful viva (Hopwood, 2010). Sometimes, PhD students working on a published work route may have a similar emotional experience to those on a traditional route, as revealed in one of my interviews (see Insider Perspective 5.1).

Doctoral 'orphans'

Reading back doctoral success stories can sometimes lead to assumptions that all has been untroubled in the student–supervisor–institutional relationship. In reality, it may be somewhat different. Lee (2008: 267) writes that, 'a supervisor can make or break a PhD student', and Wisker and Robinson (2012) remind us that not all students who start a doctoral learning journey actually succeed. While, for many, this could be for perfectly acceptable reasons (new job, geographical move, retirement), for others it can be the result of never recovering from the loss of their supervisor, or the 'benign neglect' of supervisors, or a student–supervisor mismatch (Gurr, 2001) – that is, they become doctoral orphans.

Losing a supervisor along the learning journey can feel like a major setback. Students on a traditional PhD route have a clear expectation that a Director of Studies and a second supervisor will remain with that student to successful completion. It can therefore be disappointing when job changes, staff moves or changes in research direction mean new supervisors have to be allocated. It may, indeed, be similar on a prospective published work route, when you may have a supervisor from the beginning who will advise you on the writing of your articles in the five-year enrolment period and who helps you think critically about your synthesis. Retrospective PhD by published work students would not usually meet with their key advisor for synthesis planning and viva support until enrolment, about one year before the intention of a completion date; this means that the chances of having a single major advisory disruption during the year are reduced. Indeed, the advisory circle for ongoing retrospective students is more fluid and influenced by a wider group, as the writing is developed over many years through different roles and environments.

With all the routes to PhD completion there is the risk of the loss of a supervisor. They may leave for a new job, move to another part of the country, or retire. Wisker and Robinson (2012) have explored how the research experience can be negatively influenced by the breakdown of student–supervisor communication. They also observed how, often, the permanent loss of a supervisor leads to the student becoming a 'doctoral orphan', with the subsequent impact on the student's academic identity and ability, and loss of confidence in producing a sound doctoral-level contribution to knowledge. They address the issue of students on a doctoral journey who 'lose' their supervisor and who can then become 'stuck'. This impacts negatively on self-esteem and confidence, and may lead to attrition and delay in completion (Kiley and Wisker, 2009). This, again, is more of an issue for those students on the prospective (*ab initio*) published work route.

However, the loss of a supervisor/advisor is not all doom and gloom. On the contrary, constructive relationships can be made with new supervisors in order to complete all forms of PhD research (published work or traditional thesis routes). Kiley and Wisker (2009) explored how students developed speedily as autonomous learners and grasped ownership of their research work in order to ensure their success. Initial difficulties with the transitional stage of working with a new supervisor can involve the building of a new trusting relationship and having to deal with research ideas going in new directions. One of my interviewees described how a new supervisor 'couldn't get to grips with the agreed theme' in her synthesis and how the debates about it were 'rather tortuous'. However, in the medium to longer term, a troublesome supervisory experience can actually become transformative (Kiley and Wisker, 2009). Experience of supervisory loss can mark transitions that ultimately lead to 'transformation and new learning ... about survival skills, emotional resilience and identity' (Wisker and Robinson, 2012).

Institutional support and a well-honed, speedy process to replace a supervisor (Shacham and Od-Cohen, 2009) can be vital in enhancing resilience, and in empowering ownership and success in the PhD student on all routes. Indeed, the positive functional supervision model (Lee, 2008) of collegial support and developmental interaction may often overlook some students' more negative experiences. Morris and Wisker (2011) argue that negative learning experiences with supervisors can lead to a lessening in PhD student confidence and a loss of momentum, affecting achievement, the progress of their research, their writing-up and their skills development.

If you are writing a set number of published papers within a five-year time frame (i.e. the prospective route), you will have a supervisor to see you through this intense period and that can be key to success. But remember how, if you 'lose' your supervisor, being prepared to look through a new lens, being open to new ideas, and processing and using new feedback from a different supervisor can offer new opportunities for learning – valuable life and employability skills. The moral of all this appears to be that, if you are on a prospective PhD by published work route, negative supervisory–student experiences need to be addressed and, while recognizing that being 'orphaned' temporarily from your supervisor might feel stressful, it can sometimes lead (while you are waiting for your replacement) to you adopting a more empowered and confident approach to your studies and writing.

Supervisory teams and peer support with others who are writing for publication or writing up their synthesis can be valuable at all stages of your PhD by publication journey. There has been a significant upsurge in writing on the doctoral experience, as the expansion of undergraduate courses in many countries has impacted on the numbers taking up postgraduate research degrees. One very useful key strand has been Green and Usher's work (2003) on the term 'fast supervision' – supervisory practices delivered in a context where the emphasis is placed firmly on successful, timely, completion (p. 44) to describe supervision experiences (in this case, in Australia). There is a general recognition that the student and the supervisor need to regard doctoral education as 'work' and recognize it as such, viewing the audit needs, management needs, staged processes and institutional quality assurance as integral to the PhD process (Hughes and Tight, 2013). Conversely, Owler (2010: 289) has argued that this ignores individual needs and educational development, arguing against the contemporary managerial impulse of seeing the PhD student as a 'problem to be managed'. Owler emphasizes the value of considering the individual experience of the students involved.

It is a balance – a sound infrastructure, together with clear regulations and processes, can do much to reduce an individual candidate's stress. As one of my interviewees said to me, 'the process and all its deadlines are quite reassuring actually and I really only needed to worry about being critical, being original and being focused'.

Building confidence and emotional resilience

If you have some choice over your supervisor, it is worth choosing a supervisor who can build and maintain your confidence, and offer a safe environment for critical discussion. PhD student–supervisor relationships that nurture learning generate, 'emotional scaffolding which includes the gift of confidence, the sharing of risks in the presentation of new ideas, constructive criticism and the creation of a safety zone' (Mahn and John-Steiner, 2002: 52). Confidence is critical to the supervisory relationship, immaterial to the route candidates are following, and feeling good about your supervisory relationship is not always guaranteed. The individuals I surveyed stated that supervisors 'can help you develop ideas for your synthesis and give you confidence in linking-up your ideas and building a picture'. Another comment was, 'I was allocated a supervisor who I didn't take to – they had little understanding of the published work route and didn't know how to help me look at my papers and help me feel confident that my work had a coherent thread'. This is supported by research by Ingleton and Cadman analysing the experience of international PhD students in Australia. They identified how 'interpersonal experiences of acceptance, validation and support' built their confidence and enhanced their emotional wellbeing and performance (2002: 110). Cotterall (2013), in her paper exploring emotion in the longitudinal doctoral learning experience of international PhD candidates, reveals that writing and supervision practices can be common sites of tension. Wisker and Robinson (2012) emphasize how a high level of emotional resilience appears to be key to the successful completion of a PhD by any route.

Sometimes, when you are writing for publication and are not yet ready to be formally enrolled as a PhD student, you will not have an allocated supervisor. This, in itself, involves setbacks when articles are rejected or need major revisions. Very often, key co-authors or informal advisors are hard to contact, or choose not to be involved any further. Strategies to build emotional resilience are therefore essential core behaviours for the student to develop.

▶ The experience of supervising: what do the supervisors say?

What is it like being a supervisor/advisor for a student on a published work route?

Some of my surveys of supervisors for this route revealed some interesting findings. The prospective route supervisors often worked in wider supervisory teams and linked their students to other colleagues in their research centres undertaking academic papers. They described the value of being critical friends for draft-sharing, and the value of a group of academic writing colleagues and institutional writing groups in the guiding of the prospective route students. Many described the satisfaction of supporting a candidate and helping them to map out their research direction and publications over the five-year timeline.

Most supervisors loved the opportunity to work with a candidate on the retrospective route stating that, in their supervisory role, they had the opportunity to help someone document and identify an often long-established and productive research journey. One said about retrospective candidates, 'You get to know the individual's career and there is often a fascinating story to tell and it is up to me to help them tell it.' They appeared to enjoy working with individuals who were experienced and had an established reputation within their peer communities, appreciating the fact there was the opportunity for broader discussion and less time spent on the policing of the research quality. Many remarked that there was also something rewarding about advising a candidate just for the year in which they wrote their synthesis. The satisfaction of the achievable and focused nature of the job was evident; particularly remarked on was the pleasure of supporting candidates who were imaginative, realistic about making changes and who were mature enough to develop ideas in reaction to feedback. They talked a great

---

Advice from Experience 5.1
The supervisors' views

- For the prospective route students, setting a workable plan and rough direction for the research and clarity over the prospective publications at the beginning. Supporting students to maintain momentum and commitment.
- Ensuring that the students on the prospective route are supported in publishing within the allocated time frame.
- Checking the material submitted for the synthesis has been properly peer-reviewed.
- Working through with the student (if they are on a prospective route) the evidence of peer review from editors and journals.
- Ensuring citations of students' work are gathered and analysed.
- Supporting candidates in going beyond descriptive reflective cycles in their overviews and delving into effective impact analysis.
- Keeping the student to their deadlines for synthesis submission and making sure the originality of their work and how it has contributed to the field is explicit in the final synthesis and articulated in the preparation for the viva.

deal about linking the students to other training, if necessary, particularly in time management, one-to-ones with academic writing experts, mock viva voce examinations and bibliometric advice for issues relating to research impact. Others enjoyed supporting students who were writing their synthesis at a distance through Skype and with feedback by email.

The main challenges for the supervisor on a published work route
In my surveys, I asked the supervisors what they felt were the main challenges of supervising and advising on published work routes (see Advice from Experience 5.1).

▶ **Advice from experience**

Some of the surveys received from students who completed the PhD by published work routes described ways to make the most of your supervisor (see Advice from Experience 5.2).

**Advice from Experience 5.2
How to make the most of your supervisor/
advisor**

- Have an agenda or a list of discussion points ready for each meeting with the supervisor so that you can access the information you need from each meeting.
- If you can (and your university allows you), choose your supervisors carefully; make sure they are experienced and that the lead supervisor has a good understanding of the published work route – some do not.
- Agree on a communication plan that suits both supervisors and you. Every two to three months can be an appropriate time interval.
- Review your writing plan regularly (especially if you are on a prospective route).
- If you are on the prospective route and lose your supervisor, take control of your research, keep writing to meet your deadlines, use your peers as 'critical friends' and proactively chase up a successor with the university.

---

6 Managing Your Viva Voce Examination ... and Beyond

A viva (or viva voce, meaning 'live voice') is an oral examination. There are innumerable valuable handbooks focusing on supporting students through the conventional PhD route viva voce examinations and on how to perform well in them (McMillan and Weyers, 2013; Murray, 2009; Trafford and Leshem 2002b; Wisker, 2007). This chapter will focus less on the well-known, more general advice for viva voce examinations which is readily available and, instead, will focus on the specific purpose and structure of the viva voce examination for PhD by published work routes. The worst thing to do in preparation for any viva is just hope it will 'be all right on the night'. As Race (2007) writes, 'You may deserve for it to go well but it is important to take some steps to maximise the likelihood that nothing will go wrong.' To reflect this, the chapter will focus on practical strategies to enhance the preparation for your viva and to minimize risk. It will use authentic ideas and advice from examiners, successful candidates and the supervisors.

I will show initially how the viva for published work awards is different from the traditional PhD viva and then will concentrate on advice around how to prepare to demonstrate the originality of your work and your contribution to subject knowledge, and how to articulate the impact of your work to the examiners. To help clarify expectations, I explore the 'normal' process, the examiners' roles and the value of rehearsing using a 'mock', and offer a range of authentic sample questions from candidates on published work routes which can be practised in advance of the big day. The issues of exactly what to expect on the day, the examiners' recommendations and the reality of your future work are also addressed.

▶ The same … but different

What's different about the viva voce examination for the published work route?

The typical PhD viva voce examination for conventional thesis-based routes focuses on detailed questioning around the specific methodology, analysis and findings of the presented research. In this case, the examiners need to be able to quality assure the design, methodology and understanding the student has in their subject area because the work will *not* already have been peer-reviewed for publication. On the other hand, the viva for any route for a published work candidate has a different focus. Because the work has already been peer-reviewed, published and is in the public domain, in essence, the assurance of the quality and rigour of the research has already taken place. Examiners will concentrate on the content of the synthesis and give the candidate the opportunity to articulate the original nature of their work and the impact of the publications over time. They will specifically encourage exploration of how the scholarship of the overall corpus of published work has contributed to the knowledge of their field and the development of their research journey over time.

The viva for thesis-based PhD routes will also address the contribution and originality of the work in the thesis, as these are key criteria for all PhD commensurate awards but, overall, long-term impact and holistic contribution over time cannot be measured.

Viva voce for PhD by published work routes: is it the same everywhere?

It is not a universal, global requirement for doctoral candidates to defend their thesis (either in public or in a closed examination) in order to be awarded a PhD degree, although 98 per cent of UK universities reported it as compulsory (UKCGE, 2004) for published work routes. In Australia, for example, it has never been the norm for candidates to undergo an oral examination (viva) for PhDs. The assessment can be based on the examiners reading and commenting on the candidate's work. In reality, though, some universities do instigate viva examinations. It currently seems unlikely that the UK or other European countries would wish to move to a remotely assessed model for doctoral degrees, as the defence of the thesis/published work for all PhD routes is central to the examiners being assured of the candidate's depth and breadth of knowledge and understanding, as well as the original nature of the research. This oral examination for thesis-based PhD routes also enables examiners to triangulate to check for plagiarism by questioning students on wider issues and originality. The same would apply for published work candidates but they would be based on the ideas and content of the synthesis, as the existing published papers would already have been quality assured for the public domain.

It has been argued that the research degree examination in the UK has become an affair that is somewhat shrouded in mystery, with an unclear purpose and procedures, and that a significant number of all PhD candidates are not fully aware of what is required of them in the doctoral examination (Pearce, 2005). To enhance the quality, transparency and rigour of PhD viva examinations, it is important to view the assessment of research degrees in the same way as the conduct and good practice of all good quality higher education assessment (Clarke and Powell, 2009). They discuss how the viva is, in itself, a distinctive form of assessment but that the principles of effective pedagogy, rigour and criteria-based marking should still apply consistently in its design, undertaking and conduct, as will all assessment for all levels of learning in higher education.

In many European countries, a public defence of the thesis (or the synthesis) is required. This can address any doubts about the candidate's ability to present and defend his or her arguments, at the same time thus assuring the originality of the PhD work, and the sharing and discussion of it with a wider audience. It has been suggested that UK doctoral examinations might be improved if they were more closely aligned to practice in continental Europe, although there are currently no such moves afoot to do this (QAA, 2011b).

► Preparing for your viva voce examination

Well ... you have submitted several securely bound copies of your peer-reviewed papers and outputs in a coherent area, an abstract of your research, the full synthesis, your curriculum vitae, a batch of signed co-authors' letters of confirmation and maybe a range of other artefacts and outputs. You have complied with the university submission instructions, you have proof-read the synthesis, and submitted it before the deadline and now you have to ... wait. Depending on the availability of your examiners, there may be a three-month wait before your viva. Most universities have regulations stating that all viva examinations must take place within six months of submission of the degree synthesis. How can you best make use of this waiting time?

Publishing and presenting

Can you build your confidence by using the time to practise presenting your work? Many candidates on a published work route I interviewed find the fact that they may have already had a career presenting their work at conferences generates a strong grounding in the processes operating in the wider externally-facing research culture. They described how they knew they would have to articulate ideas, justify their thinking and defend their work in the viva, and that fielding questions from conference audiences was excellent preparation for the rigours of the viva.

It appears that the whole act of having published can contribute to a 'destressing' before the viva. Wellington (2010) has identified the developmental benefits of publishing and presenting over time, including the opportunity to clarify ideas, build self-confidence and reap personal satisfaction from seeing your work in print. Taylor and Beasley (2005) and Barnacle and Mewburn (2010) have also described the benefits of a 'publish as you go' approach, and its positive impact on preparation and enhanced viva performance.

Having a mock viva voce examination

Examiners of PhD by published work viva voce examinations and the candidates themselves all recommended doing a mock exam – it gives you the opportunity to rehearse answers to key questions that will come up. It allows you as a candidate to prepare for the feeling of facing the panel, and gives you the opportunity to explain your subject and rehearse key arguments. Role-playing the difficult questions and hard-to-please examiners in non-threatening situations can prepare you for hearing the sound of your own voice, decide which points to emphasize and help you identify the areas in which you are least comfortable answering questions. It is better to know this in advance of the viva day. The PhD for publication viva voce examination will focus on originality, your contribution to the knowledge and the impact of your work – make sure you specifically include difficult and easier questions on these areas in your mock viva, and practise explaining them in different ways (and in the mirror at home on your own).

One examiner I interviewed, who was experienced in the running of viva voce examinations for published work candidates advised that, even if you do not have the opportunity to undergo a mock viva, or you choose not to have one, you should 'always have a person independent of your supervision team to read through your submitted synthesis and identify key areas for questions'. He explained how they will identify areas for questioning that you have not thought of and they will identify possible gaps that need to be filled, or inaccuracies which you may have to be prepared to defend.

University-run support for viva voce examinations

Some universities run viva preparation workshops as dress rehearsals for all their PhD candidates, whatever route they have taken. These can be a very useful way to enhance your general understanding of the process, reassure you and clarify your expectations for the day of the viva. Many candidates commented that, because of the larger numbers of candidates doing the traditional route, the format of the traditional viva tended to form most of the content of the training workshops. As a result, viva preparation for the smaller numbers of published work tended to be subsumed into this workshop, leading to a situation where the individual published work candidate's specific needs were neglected. Some universities do run specific viva preparation workshops for published work candidates on an *ad hoc* basis at times when a number of candidates are approaching the end of their synthesis write-up and are within a few months of their viva. That said, many of my interviewees were clear that the most useful institutional support workshops were at an earlier stage in the process, stating that having workshops and group advice around sufficiency, collation of papers, honing down and selecting papers from the entire body of work for the final submission around a theme was more helpful.

▶ Answering the examiners' questions

The key thrust of the questions will focus on *originality*, *impact* and *contribution to knowledge*. These areas will be discussed in depth in your synthesis and you must prepare this thoroughly prior to the viva by re-reading these sections so that you are on top of the content.

Originality
This is the big question. You will need to discuss the originality clearly in your synthesis and then be prepared to defend it in your viva. The concept of 'originality' is different for PhDs by publication compared with the traditional PhD by thesis route. The key difference is that your work may have been published slowly over many years. What was 'new' when your first paper was published 10 years ago will not be new and original now! This does not matter, but you need to be able to show how your work *was* original at the time of publication.

The content of the submitted papers appended to your synthesis will illuminate this and the content of the synthesis itself should include a summary outline reflecting on the originality of each paper published. A summary of how the work has moved on should also be included in the synthesis. You can use this evidence to prepare for the viva. Your work needs to show that it is new and your viva defence will need to prove that it was original in comparison with the literature as it existed at the time.

During the viva you might be asked questions such as:

* What makes your work original?
* Why was your first submitted paper original at the time?
* What do you consider your main contribution to your practice area to be now?

You might also be asked what others have written since about your work. Have you been cited in papers by other authors? What follow-on work have you done which moves original earlier work forward?

Impact analysis
You may also be asked to discuss the impact of your work. This should have been outlined in your synthesis and you will need to prepare for this. There is a detailed account in Chapter 3 of ways you can analyse the impact of your work. You will need to be prepared (if asked) to discuss citations' indices, how your work has influenced others, testimonials, sales figures of books (if appropriate), or whether you have been invited as a keynote speaker to a major conference as a follow-up to any of your published work.

Your corpus of work: contribution to knowledge over time?
Unlike a traditional PhD, when the viva concentrates on your defence of the thesis of your work, a published work viva will encapsulate questions about your research journey over many years and many publications. You will need to be able to explain to the examiners how your series of research projects, your underpinning theoretical and conceptual frameworks, activities and artefacts have been informed by the subject and the context, and how research and emergent ideas have changed *over time*. Research into doctoral viva voce examinations for all PhD routes shows that examiners place importance on the significance, role and use of theory and how that has informed the contribution to knowledge overall (Trafford and Leshem, 2002a; 2000b). Your submitted synthesis will have explored your conceptual framework and you will need to articulate this to your examiners. You should prepare to be able to address the following questions: What is the theoretical background? How has this acted as scaffolding for your research process? Who are your key theoretical influences and what are your overall research paradigms over time? How have your conceptual frameworks informed your output, findings and ongoing work?

As Lewin (1952) expressed, 'There is nothing so practical as a good theory.' Conceptual frameworks can really help you develop useful generalizations about the overall impact of your work. As Rudestam and Newton

(1992: 7) noted, 'Generalisations are made on the basis of the particular data that have been observed and are tied to a conceptual framework which then leads to the elucidation of further research questions and implications for additional study.' It is clear that explaining the notion of a conceptual framework (i.e. the intellectual thinking on which your work is based) needs thought and preparation (Burton and Steane, 2005) whether this be for thesis-based routes, or for the more integrated holistic thinking required for published work awards.

If you have left it until the day of your viva to consider this ... it is too late. All this thinking should be embedded in the content of your synthesis. Failure to include a consideration of the intellectual or theoretical underpinning of your work and the research questions which were generated from its consideration will fail to meet the requirements of 'doctoralness' and so will be unlikely to pass (Leshem and Trafford, 2007). You need to able to say confidently and clearly how your work fully constitutes a doctoral body of work. An examiner I interviewed was quite clear that this was absolutely the key issue saying 'it's not the examiners' job to read everything and figure this out for themselves – it is up to the candidate to explain the links.'

Speaking to another examiner of a PhD by published work route, she said that her favourite initial question was to ask the candidate to tell them about their 'research journey', as this illuminates the chronology and progress of the subject, and the candidate's view of it over time. You need to be prepared for a question like this. You may be asked where the key areas of originality are *as part of* this research journey question. Indeed, this might not be in the most recent work, so you need to look back over your timeline and be prepared to talk about the originality of your earlier work and how it catalysed a series of ideas which have been developed either singly or with others. The mind mapping ideas outlined in Chapter 3 may help with this.

Your later papers submitted to support your synthesis may be expanding on a theme – the equivalent of a post-doctoral publication – and you should be able to explain and defend them. You will be assessed on your ability *as an independent researcher* to explain the strengths and weaknesses of your body of work, to elucidate each paper's contribution at every stage and whether they have impacted on policy, pedagogy, or practice. You may well be asked about any future research you intend to do that builds on this. To be able to do this well in the viva means you must have a clear understanding and critical overview of the whole nature of your body of work and its coherence, contribution and originality.

▶ The role of the examiners

The examiners will address all aspects of your PhD by published work but, essentially, they have to satisfy themselves that it is your own original work, that it meets the requirements for a PhD by published work at your university and, specifically, that it makes a significant contribution to knowledge in a particular academic field. The publications also provide evidence that the examiner can be assured that you can pursue further research without supervision (Open University, 2013).

The material submitted must represent a coherent contribution to research in your academic field at a level and scope equivalent to that of a conventional PhD thesis. For most PhD awards, this examination would usually have at least two examiners, often three examiners – the requirement in the UK is usually (a Chair – internal, one other internal examiner and an examiner from an external institution) (QAA, 2011a). If you are an internal candidate and undertaking a PhD by published work award at your university, you would usually have three examiners (a Chair – internal, and two external examiners). Panels need to be approved by your university's Research Awards Committee, or its equivalent, prior to the confirmation of the viva. (See Insider Perspective 6.1, which describes the difficulties of finding an external examiner.)

University regulations and practice do appear to vary in relation to how much choice you have over panel membership. Your supervisor/advisor might ask you for two or three experts in your field who you would be happy to invite to the viva and then recommend them to your University Awards Committee. It is unlikely that a colleague from another university with whom you have co-authored will be approved by your Awards Committee as your external examiner. This is because your viva, as part of the research degree, must be quality assured for externality and lack of bias is integral to this. The external examiners may be individuals you have referenced in your synthesis and in some of your peer-reviewed published work. Sometimes, the title of

---

Insider Perspective 6.1 Finding an external examiner for your viva voce examination

Sometimes it is quite hard as you are very likely to have worked (or co-published) with people in your field and you can't use them as an external. Ideally, you want an external you have referenced, who knows your work but with whom you have not actually co-published.

Current PhD by published work candidate, UK

your synthesis and identified 'golden thread' can be quite broad and conceptual, and a variety of people might have contributed to your thinking. Your
Director of Studies might well be specifically subject-based and for example,
you might want to have an external with a more conceptual or holistic
knowledge of practice in that area. Or, indeed, your supervisor might have
'breadth' and you might have a panel that contains an external with specific
subject knowledge about your methodology or specific findings. Your own
supervisor/advisor may be allowed to attend the viva voce examination but
cannot contribute to the discussion. They may be in attendance and can
write notes about your performance which they can use for feedback after
the event. This can be particularly valuable if you have some revisions to
make.

The whole panel has to be approved prior to confirmation of your viva
date. The proposed external examiners have to submit their curriculum
vitae and outline their research experience to the candidate's university to
assess their suitability and relevant knowledge. Very often, they will have
supervised and examined all types of PhDs and professional doctorates, and
have experience of asking questions at the right level and depth in the
examination of your PhD by published work – that is, not assessing the
quality of the publications but, rather, asking you to defend its originality,
impact and contribution to the wider field. Availability of external examiners can be tricky to confirm and, sometimes, if a particular external expert is
required, you might have to be prepared to wait longer for your viva. It
appeared from my work that, in the UK, the average length of time between
submission of the synthesis and the viva voce examination date was four to
five months.

▶ On the day

What will happen?

Viva voce panels (the Chair and the internal and external examiners) will
usually have a pre-meeting on the day of your viva at which they will discuss
the quality of your submitted synthesis. They may already have been asked
to send in a report of comments to form the framework for discussion. They
will be asked to discuss whether the combination of the body of work *plus*
the content and thinking in the synthesis is at the same standard and at a
commensurate level to a thesis submitted through the traditional thesis-
based route. The panel will then allocate questions according to areas of
your synthesis they may wish to probe further. The internal examiners (and
especially the Chair) may have to guide new external examiners on the

Insider Perspective 6.2 The panel for the viva voce examination

Some new external examiners are tempted to treat the viva for PhD by existing body of work the same as for a traditional PhD and it is not quite the same. The examiners are not on the panel to seek a defence of the quality, rigour and findings of the research like they would be for a traditional PhD – that is the job of the peer-review quality assurance process that has already taken place at the journal. The examiners at this kind of viva are there to ask questions about the research journey and seek reassurance that the body of work is thematic, original, cohesive, is contextualized to a wider literature and points to new directions of study for the self-reflecting candidate. They only have 10,000 words of the synthesis to help them judge whether a PhD should be awarded (unlike the 80,000 to 100,000 words in a traditional thesis) so I know it is in the interests of the candidate to write their synthesis tightly and effectively, particularly reflecting the research journey, coherence, thematic and originality issues.

Professor and examiner successfully completed PhD by published work (retrospective route)

process. Indeed, many of my interviewees stated how difficult it was to find examiners who were experienced and familiar with undertaking viva examinations for the published work route. One of my interviewees talked about this issue (see Insider Perspective 6.2).

Regulations about whether you are allowed to take an annotated copy of the synthesis into the viva vary, and you should check your specific regulations. Most viva voce examinations for this route varied from between 45 minutes to two hours and it can be a 'full on' intense experience. Use all the tried and tested experience you have gleaned from many years of presenting and explaining your work to colleagues and conference audiences to do yourself real justice when facing this final hurdle.

What will the examiners ask?
Because the work in the submission is already in the published domain and peer-reviewed, the viva questions will concentrate mostly on the originality, coherence and impact of the overall body of work and its contribution to knowledge *as addressed in the synthesis*. It is highly unlikely you will be asked to do a formal presentation on your work. As one experienced examiner said, 'it is less likely to be a grilling about the detailed content of each paper, although impact will be discussed, but more a "high ground" and "big picture" discussion on (the work's) originality, impact and coherence'. In addition, we discussed how retrospective analysis of qualitative papers/outputs especially

(and its inclusion in the narrative of the synthesis) distorts or enhances 'one version of the truth' and whether it could be perceived to be biased. (See Box 6.1 for examples of questions used for a PhD by published work viva voce examination.)

Box 6.1   Examples of questions used for a PhD by published work viva voce examination

Examples of questions that a panel may ask at your viva:

- Can you tell us about your research journey?
- Who are your key theoretical influences? What theories link and underpin your work? Have any new theorists been influential in the latter/earlier stages of your work and how have they informed your thinking? Have they generated any new research questions which you have then used in any of your publications? Can you give some examples?
- How have your conceptual frameworks influenced your outputs, findings, generalizability and ongoing work?
- Explain your themes? How do they contribute to the overall body of knowledge in this area? Where do you think the gaps still are? Has your work filled any of these gaps at any point?
- What was the relative impact of each article? How do you know this and what happened after each one?
- Can you highlight the coherence of each article and how one paper led to another?
- We can see you have taken a particular approach with your methodology in your published papers. Would you stick with this in the future? What has it added to your overall approach?
- Why do you think your work is original? What was original about it at the time each paper/output was published and what is your overall 'end point' feeling about the originality of your work today, prior to any new work taking place?
- What is the one version of the truth? The inclusion of your reflection is your view retrospectively. Is that more or less accurate or biased? How does it influence and affect the validity?
- What do you see might be the limitations of your overall body of work and how might you want to address this in future directions for your research?

▶ At the end of your PhD by published work viva voce examination

The recommendations available to examiners

University regulations vary from institution to institution but, basically, examiners have three decisions:

- They will recommend the award of a degree of PhD by published work.
- They will recommend the award of a degree of PhD by published work subject to specified revisions in the synthesis. Or, rarely:
- They will recommend that the degree is not awarded. Any new application would require re-registration, a substantially new submission of the synthesis, or a full review of the coherence of the submitted papers.

Major modifications to a synthesis following viva for the PhD by publication route are rare, provided that the published outputs have been selected rigorously and the coherence and originality clearly articulated in the synthesis. From my surveys of post-viva published work candidates who had some revisions to do to their synthesis, most focused on the following matters:

- Making the synthesis more concise.
- Explaining the contribution to knowledge and theoretical linkage in more depth in the synthesis.
- Articulating the originality element more clearly to mirror the content of the viva discussion.
- Enhancing the generalizability of the themes in the synthesis to other populations and the wider community.
- Editing issues.
- Clarification to the content of the abstract.

▶ Your future work

When does the PhD by publication ever really finish? Is it just a milestone in the longer-term process of your ongoing research career? Prospective route published work PhD students are often earlier in their career than the retrospective candidates who may be submitting their work towards the end of a long and active research career. There is no rule that you have to carry on researching after your PhD. But, if you love research, enjoy publishing and need to publish as part of your academic career, then there is no real reason to stop. That said, many individuals said they 'took a deep breath' after their viva and 'temporarily switched off with relief'. Who would blame them?

The people I researched who had completed their PhD by existing published work retrospectively at the end of their career had gained great satisfaction from reviewing their corpus of work. They intended to continue promoting their subject, networking, attending conferences and contributing research to their area. Many (in all routes) stated how having a PhD acted as a springboard for future work and new career opportunities, and gave them status and confidence from knowing they had contributed to their subject field.

▶ Endnote

This book has aimed to show you that attaining a PhD by published work is achievable and that, to a certain extent, the joy of inquiry, writing, co-authoring and publishing over many years means that you can gradually establish yourself as a credible researcher. You can make contacts, integrate with research groups in your subject and professional areas, and slowly build your profile alongside the teaching, scholarly and leadership commitments which are part of your wider academic career.

This more gradual approach to attaining a PhD suits many who find it less daunting and more developmental – this approach allowing research-led insights to build and evidence to grow and accumulate over time. This step-wise approach can seem more satisfying, as the impact and influence of a corpus of work can be honed and formed over many years, and described to examiners with the authenticity and consistency gained from this longer view. In parallel, with each successful peer-reviewed publication comes greater self-esteem and confidence. Achieving the PhD will give you great personal satisfaction, but it might not (and perhaps should not) change your existing daily research ethos and activity, especially if your love of researching and publishing, and a passion for your subject area, is in your blood. Many PhD by published work scholars who had successfully completed the journey told me that their ongoing work life was 'business as usual' ... but that it was 'good business!'

Appendix
Completed Examples of an Activity Template

This Appendix presents two completed examples of using an activity template with supervisor/advisor comments and planning goals. They may help you identify whether you have enough acceptable work and help you plan your goals. The first example (Table A.1, pp. 144–5) has been completed by an academic staff member in the UK contemplating doing a PhD via publishing an existing published work. She is an early career research academic and in a science-related field.

Table A.1 Example of a completed activity template (1)

Where are you now? Are you en route to a PhD by published work?	Number of publications for submission and theme identification
Do you have a wider body of peer-reviewed work from which you can select some papers around a core theme(s)?	
How many *single-authored papers* in peer-reviewed journals have you got in total?	2
Are they all around a *core theme*?	YES – it relates to the challenges of clinical teaching in a science/health specialism
How many have you got on a *core theme*?	2
How many *joint-authored papers* in peer-reviewed journals?	1
Are they all around a *core theme*?	YES – the same one as above
How many have you got on a *core theme*?	1
How many peer-reviewed book chapters have you got? Does your university count them?	One. Yes, they count them as they are peer-reviewed.
Are they all around the same *core theme*?	Yes
If YES, How many chapters have you got on a *core theme*?	1
Does your university allow conference papers, films, performance, exhibits, artefacts or teaching materials/resources as part of the submission?	No
If YES, how many of these high-quality artefacts have you got?	N/A
Look at your regulations for PhD by published work. What's your current useful total so far?	4
How many more of each do you need? **Papers** **Book chapters** **Other artefacts (conference papers, reviews, media, exhibits, learning resources – check your regulations to see what is allowed)**	Maybe 6 more papers of which at least 4–5 should be single-authored
Give this form to an academic mentor/potential supervisor for advice and comment	

→

Advisor's comments (please complete below)

The regulations for our University only accept book chapters and peer-reviewed publications. I know some Unis have a broader definition of the kind of submissions which are acceptable. This potential candidate needs to really write another. We need about 8–10 papers of which the majority should be single authored so I would say this candidate can carry on writing jointly but needs at least another 4–5 – should be single authored. Some additional joint papers (2–4) around the key theme should suffice. Try and target some journals that relate more to your core theme or some new journals focussing on academic practice. They usually have a faster turnaround time and so might speed things up for you. It is good you are writing to a core theme from an early stage. Less chance your work is wasted but be careful you don't blinker yourself to new ideas while over concentrating on one thing. You only have one book chapter – can you submit 2 more of these – where you can show that there is a peer-review process – perhaps with a letter from the editor?

Again, make these chapters linked to the core theme. Try and link them to the research work you are already doing (perhaps your supervisor or colleagues are already working on books and need an additional contribution in your research area?) and maybe write a summary article around your key theme towards the end of the process? We might allow some supplementary supporting material like abstract or conference presentations to show you are applying and disseminating your work but this would not be part of the core assessed submission. There is a lot of work to be done here over quite a long period of time before you would be in a position to write your synthesis but set yourself some publication goals and you should be able to do it.

In the light of the comments above, what's your action plan?

Set some achievable publishing goals with a colleague/ mentor/potential supervisor.

In the next 2 months I need to have

- **Identified some key journals which will publish work around my core theme.**

In the longer term (in the next twelve months)

- **I need to have at least two more papers accepted (sole and joint) and start developing the confidence to submit more sole authored papers.**
- **See if I can contribute to or offer to write a sole book chapter on my existing work.**

The second example (see Table A.2) has been completed by a mid-career academic in a creative field in Australia undertaking her PhD by published work through a retrospective route. You will see that her supervisor advises she has considerably more work to do and is not so well-advanced in the process.

Table A.2 Example of a completed activity template (2)

Where are you now? Are you en route to a PhD by published work?	*Number of publications for submission and theme identification*
Do you have a wider body of peer-reviewed work which you can select some papers around a core theme(s)?	Yes
How many *single authored papers* in peer-reviewed journals have you got in total?	4
Are they all around a *core theme*?	NO – I don't think so
How many have you got on a *core theme*?	Maybe 2 though don't really have an absolutely clear idea yet what my core theme is.
How many *joint authored papers* in peer-reviewed journals?	1
Are they all around a *core theme*?	Possibly.
How many have you got on a *core theme*?	I think I can make links between 2 of the papers I have done on my own.
How many book chapters have you got?	None.
Are they all around a *core theme*?	N/A.
If YES, How many have you got on a *core theme*?	N/A
Does your university allow conference papers, films, performance, exhibits, artefacts or teaching materials/resources as part of the submission?	YES as part of a primarily written peer-reviewed portfolio they will accept.
If YES, how many of these high quality artefacts have you got?	I have some exhibited sculpture which was selected for a major national exhibition.

→

What's your current useful total?	Probably the sculpture and 2 single papers. The joint paper might count if I could link it to my theme. I doubt it though.

How many more of each do you need?
   Papers
   Book chapters
   **Other artefacts* (conference papers, reviews,
   media, exhibits, learning resources – check your
   regulations to see what is allowed)**
	At the University where I want to work they need 7 peer-reviewed publications. I think I need four more papers (co-authored or sole) and perhaps two artefacts. They don't allow book chapters.

You could give this form to an academic mentor/potential supervisor for advice and comment **Advisor's comments (please complete below).** I think there is quite a lot more work to do here and her calculation is realistic. We don't allow book chapters. If this individual is focused on gaining a PhD by Publication then identification of a core theme and sticking to it with more joint and single authored publications is key. Initially she should work with a colleague to try to identify a strong clear intellectual theme and stick to it. Where do the 2 other single authored papers sit? Are they on an entirely different theme? It might be worth adding to the submission with more art exhibitions in the public domain which can be documented as a permanent record if the University regulations permit that, as this is part of her 'work in progress on a daily basis' and may link well with her core theme. Perhaps she should join an academic writing group and seek out new and very subject specific journals which will publish her work. It is the lack of coherence here which is the big issue.	
In the light of the comments above, what's your action plan? **Can you set some achievable publishing goals with a colleague/mentor/potential supervisor?** In the short term (approximately the next 3 months) I need to:	

→

- Meet with one of my colleagues to help me identify my core theme related to my active research interests and original ideas and do a plan of additional work needed and what artwork already in the public domain I can use.
- Sign up to the University writing group and use it to help me.
- Once I have identified my theme and plan start writing sole authored papers and stick to the deadline.

In the next year I need to:

- Have written up elements of my research into at least 2 sole authored papers around a coherent theme and submit these for peer review at appropriate journals.

References

Adams, J. (2013) 'Collaborations: The fourth age of research', *Nature*, 497: 557–60.

Antelman, K. (2004) 'Do Open Access Articles have a greater research impact?', *College and Research Libraries News*, 65(5): 372–82.

Arkoudis, S. and Tran, L. (2010) 'Writing blah, blah, blah: Lecturers' approaches and challenges in supporting international students, *International Journal of Teaching and Learning in Higher Education*, 22(2): 169–78.

Barnacle, R. and Mewburn, I. (2010) 'Learning networks and the journey of "becoming doctor"', *Studies in Higher Education*, 35: 433–44.

Barnett, R. (1997) *Higher Education: A Critical Business.* (Buckingham: Open University Press).

Bastow, S., Dunleavy, P., and Tinkler, J. (2014) *The Impact of the Social Sciences: How Academics and Their Research Make a Difference* (London: Sage).

Beel, J., Gipp, B., and Stiller, J. (2009) 'Information Retrieval on Mind Maps – what could it be good for?', *Proceedings of the 5th International Conference on Collaborative Computing: Networking, Applications and Work-sharing* (CollaborateCom'09), Washington, IEEE.

Berlin, J.A. (1982) 'Contemporary composition: The major pedagogical theories', *College English*, 44(8): 765–77.

Boud, D. and Lee, A. (2008) *Changing Practices in Doctoral Education* (London: Routledge).

Brown, K. and Cooke, C. (2010) *Professional Doctorate Awards in the UK* (Lichfield: UK Council for Graduate Education)

Burton, S. and Steane, P. (eds) (2005) *Surviving your Thesis* (London: Routledge).

Buzan, T. (1974) *Use Your Head* (London: BBC Books).

Caffarella, R.S. and Barnett, B.G. (2000) 'Teaching doctoral students to become scholarly writers: the importance of giving and receiving critiques', *Studies in Higher Education*, 25(1): 39–51.

Carter, S. (2009) 'Old lamps for new: Mnemonic techniques and the thesis structure', *Arts and Humanities in Education*, 8: 56–68.

Carter, S., Kelly, F. and Brailsford, I. (2012) *Structuring Your Research Thesis*, Palgrave Research Skills (Basingstoke: Palgrave Macmillan).

Castello, M., Inesta, A. and Monereo, C. (2009) 'Towards self-regulated academic writing: An exploratory study with graduate students in a situated learning environment', *Electronic Journal of Research in Educational Psychology*, 7(3): 1107–30.

Chickering, A.W. and Gamson, Z.F. (1987) 'Seven principles for good practice in undergraduate education', *American Association of Higher Education Bulletin*, 39(7): 3–7.

Clarke, G. and Powell, S. (2009) *Quality and Standards of Postgraduate Research Degrees* (UK Council for Graduate Education).

Clegg, S., Tan, J. and Saedi, S. (2002) 'Reflecting or acting? Reflective practice and continuing professional development in higher education, *Reflective Practice*, 3(1): 131–46.

Cohen, L. and Manion, L. (2000) *Research Methods in Education* (5th edn) (London: Routledge): 254.

Cooke, E (2013) 'Spider diagrams: how and why they work', Telegraph Education, *Daily Telegraph* (Online), 2 February. Available from: http://www.telegraph.co.uk/education/educationadvice/9839678/Spider-diagrams-how-and-why-they-work.html (accessed 8 June 2014).

Costas, R., Zahedi, Z. and Wouters, P. (2014) 'Do altmetrics correlate with citations? Extensive comparison of altmetric indicators with citations from a multidisciplinary perspective' *Journal of the Association for Information Science and Technology*: 1–30.

Cotterall, S. (2013) 'More than just a brain: Emotions and the doctoral experience', *Higher Education Research and Development*, 32(2): 174–87.

Creswell, J. and Tashakkori, A. (2007) 'Differing perspectives on mixed methods research', *Journal of Mixed Methods Research*, 1: 303–8.

Cumming, J. (2010) 'Doctoral enterprise: A holistic conception of evolving practices and arrangements', *Studies in Higher Education*, 35: 25–39.

Davis, L. and McKay, S. (1996) *Structures and Strategies: An Introduction to Academic Writing* (South Yarra: Macmillan).

Delasalle, J. and Goodall, J. (2013) *Co-authorship and Attribution – University of Warwick* (Online). Available from: www.slideshare.net/jdelasalle/co-authorship-and-attribution (accessed 1 May 2014).

Department for Education and Skills (2007) 'Bologna Process Stocktaking Report', London (Online). Available from: http://www.ond.vlaanderen.be/hgeronderwijs/bologna/documets/WGR2007/Stcktaking_report2007.pdf (accessed 1 May 2014).

Dick, B. (1997) 'Approaching an action research thesis: an overview', *Resource papers in action research* (Online). Available from: http://www.uq.net.au/action/arp/phd.html (accessed 8 June 2014).

Donnelly, R. (2014) 'Supporting lecturers in the disciplines in the affective academic writing process', *Journal of Academic Writing*, 4(1): 26–39.

Draper, S. W. (2012) *PhDs by publication* (Online). Available from: http://www. psy.gla.ac.uk/~steve/resources/phd.html (accessed 11 April 2014).

Dyke, M. (2006) 'The role of the "Other" in reflection, knowledge formation and action in a late modernity', *International Journal of Lifelong Education*, 25(2): 105–23.

Emig, J. (1977) 'Writing as a mode of learning', *College Composition and Communication*, 28(2): 122–8.

Evans, T. (2010) 'Understanding Doctoral Research for Professional Practitioners', in Walker, M. and Thompson, P. (eds), *The Routledge Doctoral Supervisor's Companion* (London and New York: Routledge): 65–75.

Feldman, A. (2008) 'Does academic culture support translational research?', *CTS: Clinical and Translational Sciences* (Online), 1(2): 87–8. Available from: http://ccts.uth.tmc.edu/what-is-translational-research (accessed 3 April 2013).

Felton, S. (2008) 'Why Do a Postgraduate Research Degree?', in Hall, G. and Longman, J. (eds), *The Postgraduate's Companion* (London: Sage).

Finch Report (2012) 'Accessibility, Sustainability, Excellence: How to Expand Access to Research Publications', *Report of the Working group on Expanding Access to Published Research Findings*, Finch Group, Research Information Network.

Flores, E. and Nerad, M. (2012) 'Peers in doctoral education: Unrecognized partners', *New Directions for Higher Education*, 157, Spring: 73–83.

Fook, J. (2004) 'Critical Reflection and Organisational Learning and Change', in Gould, N. and Baldwin, M. (eds), *Social Work, Critical Reflection and the Learning Organisation* (Aldershot and Burlington: Ashgate).

Freidson, E. (1986) *Professional Powers: A Study of the Institutionalisation of Formal Knowledge* (University of Chicago Press).

Freire, P. (1968) *Pedagogy of the Oppressed* (London: Penguin Books).

Ghaye, T. (2005) *Developing the Reflective Healthcare Team* (Oxford: Blackwell Publishing).

Gilliver, S. (2013) '7 Tips for Dealing with Reviewer Comments', ECR2STAR conference (Online). Available from: http://ecr2star.org/blog/2013/10/15/7-secrets-for-dealing-with-reviewer-comments (accessed on 3 March 2014).

Glaser, B. (1998) *Doing Grounded Theory-Issues and Discussions* (Mill Valley, CA: Sociology Press).

Glaser, B.G. and Strauss A.L. (1999) *The Discovery of Grounded Theory: Strategies for Qualitative Research* (New York: Aldine de Gruyter).

Government White Paper (1993) *Realising Our Potential: A Strategy for Science, Engineering and Technology* (London: HMSO).

Grant, C. (2011) 'Diversifying and transforming the doctoral studies terrain: A student's experience of a thesis by publication', *Alternation*, 18(2): 245–67.

Green, B. (2009) 'Challenging Perspectives, Changing Practices: Doctoral Education in Transition', in Boud, D and Lee, A. (eds), *Changing Practices of Doctoral Education* (London: Routledge).

Green, H. and Powell, S. (2005) *Doctoral Study in Contemporary Higher Education* (Buckingham: Open University Press).

Green, P. and Usher, R. (2003) 'Fast supervision: Changing supervisory practice in changing times', *Studies in Continuing Education*, 25(1): 37–50.

Gurr, G. (2001) 'Negotiating "the rackety bridge." A dynamic model for aligning supervisory style with research student development', *Higher Education and Development*, 20(1): 81–92.

Halse, C. and Malfoy, J. (2010) 'Retheorizing doctoral supervision as professional work', *Studies in Higher Education*, 35: 79–92.

Harman, K.M. (2008) 'Challenging Traditional Research Training Culture: Industry Oriented Doctoral Programs in Australian Cooperative Research Centres', in Välimaa, J. and Ylijoki, O.-H. (eds), *Cultural Perspectives on Higher Education* (London: Springer Books)

HEFCE (Higher Education Funding Council for England) (2011) 'PhD Study: Trends and Profiles 1996–97 to 2009–10', Higher Education Funding Council Report.

Hofstadter, D. (1979) *Gödel, Escher, Bach: An Eternal Golden Braid* (New York: Basic Books).

Hirsch, J.E. (2005) 'An Index to Quantify an Individual's Scientific Research Output', *Proceedings of the National Academy of Sciences of the United States of America*, 102(46): 16569–72.

Hopwood, N. (2010) 'A sociocultural view of doctoral students' relationships and agency', *Studies in Continuing Education*, 32(2): 103–17.

Hughes, C. and Tight, M. (2013) 'The metaphors we study by: The doctorate as a journey and/or as work', *Higher Education Research and Development*, 32(5): 765–75.

ICMJE (International Committee of Medical Journal Editors) (2013) *Recommendations for the Conduct, Reporting, Editing and Publication of Scholarly Work in Medical Journals*, Updated December 2013.

Ingleton, C. and Cadman, K. (2002) 'Silent issues for international postgraduate research students: Emotion and agency in academic success', *Australian Educational Researcher*, 29(1): 93–113.

Jefferson, T., Alderson P., Wager, E. and Davidoff, F. (2002) 'Effects of editorial peer review: A systematic review', *Journal of the American Medical Association (JAMA)*, 287: 2784–6.

Kamler, B. and Thomson, P. (2006) *Helping Doctoral Students Write: Pedagogies for Supervision* (London: Routledge).

Katzenbach J.R. and Smith, D.K. (1993) *The Wisdom of Teams: Creating of High Performance Organisation* (New York: Harper Business).

Keeling, R. (2006) 'The Bologna Process and the Lisbon Research Agenda: The European Commission's expanding role in higher education discourse', *European Journal of Education,* 41(2): 203–23.

Kiley, M. and Wisker, G. (2009) 'Threshold concepts in research education and evidence of threshold crossing', *Higher Education Research Development,* 28(4): 431–41.

Kolb, D.A. (1984) *Experiential Learning Experience as a Source of Learning and Development* (New Jersey: Prentice Hall).

Lee, A. (2008) 'How are doctoral students supervised? Concepts of doctoral research supervision', *Studies in Higher Education,* 33(3): 267–81.

Lee, A. (2010) 'When the Article is the Dissertation: Pedagogies for a PhD by Publication', in Aitchison, C., Kamler, B. and Lee, A. (eds), *Publishing Pedagogies for the Doctorate and Beyond* (London: Routledge).

Lee, A. (2011) 'Professional Practice and Doctoral Education: Becoming a Researcher', in Scanlon. L. (ed.), *"Becoming" a Professional: An Interdisciplinary Analysis of Professional Learning,* Lifelong Learning Book Series, 16: 153–69 (London: Springer).

Lee, A. (2013) 'New development: Are our doctoral programmes doing what we think they are?', *Public Money and Management,* 33(2): 119–22.

Lee, A. and Kamler, B. (2008) 'Rethinking doctoral publication practices: Writing from and beyond the thesis', *Studies in Higher Education,* 33: 283–94.

Leshem, S. and Trafford, V. (2007) 'Overlooking the conceptual framework', *Innovations in Education and Teaching International,* 44(1): 93–105.

Lewin, K. (1952) *Field Theory in Social Science* (London: Tavistock).

Lupton, D. (1998) *The Emotional Self: A Sociocultural Exploration* (Thousand Oaks, CA: Sage).

Mahn, H. and John-Steiner, V. (2002) 'The Gift of Confidence: A Vygotskian View of Emotions', in Wells, G. and Claxton, G. (eds), *Learning for Life in the Twenty-first Century: Sociocultural Perspectives on the Future of Education* (Oxford: Blackwell):46–58.

Maiden, J. (2013) 'Postgraduate English Journal Forum' (Online). Available at: http://www.dur.ac.uk/postgraduate.english/forum/?page_id=135 (accessed on 3 March 2014).

Manathunga, C., Pitt, R. and Critchley, C. (2009) 'Graduate attribute development: and employment outcomes: tracking PhD graduates', *Assessment and Evaluation in Higher Education,* 34(1): 91–103.

McMillan, K. and Weyers, J. (2013) *How to Write and Research a Successful PhD* (1st edn) (London: Pearson).

Mechan-Schmidt, F. (2012) 'Excellence – but those missing out don't see it that way', *Times Higher Education,* 1 March.

Miller, B. (2010) 'Skills for sale: What is being commodified in higher education?', *Journal of Further and Higher Education,* 4: 199–206.

Moon, J. (1999) *Reflection in Learning and Professional Development* (London: Kogan Page).

Morley, L., Leonard, D. and David, M. (2003) 'Quality and equality in British PhD assessment', *Quality Assurance in Education*, 11: 64–72.

Morris, C. and Wisker, G. (2011) *ESCalate Interim Report* (York, UK: Higher Education Academy).

Morse, J.M. (2003) 'Principles of Mixed Methods and Multi-methods Research Design', In Tashakkori, A and Teddlie, C. (eds), *Handbook of Mixed Methods in Social and Behavioural Research* (Thousand Oaks, CA: Sage).

Murray, R. (2009) *How to Survive Your Viva: Defending a Thesis in an Oral Examination* (2nd edn), Open UP Study Skills (Maidenhead: Open University Press).

Murray, R. (2013) *Writing for Academic Journals* (3rd edn) (Maidenhead: McGraw-Hill International).

Nerad, M. (2004) 'The PhD in the US: Criticism, facts, and remedies', *Higher Education Policy*, 17: 183–99.

Nerad, M. (2012) 'Conceptual approaches to doctoral education: A community of Practice', *Alternation*, 19(2): 57–72 (Online). Available at: http://alternation.ukzn.ac.za/docs/19.2/04%20Ner.pdf (accessed 3 May 2014).

Niven, P. and Grant, C. (2012) 'PhDs by publications: An "easy way out"?', *Teaching in Higher Education*, 17(1): 105–11.

Nyquist, J.D. (2002) 'The PhD: A Tapestry of Change for the 21st Century', *Change: The Magazine of Higher Learning*, 34(6): 12–20.

Open University (2013) *Doctor of Philosophy by Published Work. Guidelines for Candidates*, March, Research Degrees Office.

O'Sullivan, I. and Cleary, L. (2014) 'Peer-tutoring in academic writing: The infectious nature of engagement', *Journal of Academic Writing*, 4(1): 52–65.

Owler, K. (2010) 'A "problem" to be managed? Completing a PhD in the arts and humanities', *Arts and Humanities in Higher Education*, 9(3): 289–304.

Paré, A. (2010) 'Slow the Presses: Concerns about Premature Publication', in Aitchinson, C., Kamler, B. and A Lee (eds), *Publishing Pedagogies for the Doctorate and Beyond* (New York: Routledge): 30–46.

Park, C. (2005) 'New variant PhD: The changing nature of the doctorate in the UK', *Journal of Higher Education Policy and Management*, 27(2): 189–207.

Park, C. (2007) *Redefining the Doctorate* (York: Higher Education Academy).

Pearce, L. (2005) *How to Examine a Thesis* (Maidenhead: Open University Press).

Pekrun, R., Goetz, T., Titz, W., and Perry R.P. (2002) 'Academic emotions in students' self-regulated learning and achievement: a program of qualitative and quantitative research', *Educational Psychologist*, 37(2): 91–105.

Pendlebury, D.A. (2008) *Using Bibliometrics in Evaluating Research*. Thomson Reuters, White Paper (Online). Available from: http://researchanalytics.

thomsonreuters.com/m/pdfs/Pendlebury_Paper.pdf (accessed 17 January 2014).

Powell, S. and Green, H. (2007) *The Doctorate Worldwide* (Maidenhead: Open University Press).

Piwowar, H. (2013) 'Altmetrics: What, why and where. Introduction', *Bulletin of the American Society for Information and Technology*, 39(4): 8–9.

QAA (Quality Assurance Agency) (2008) *The Framework for Higher Education Qualifications in England, Wales and Northern Ireland*, Quality Assurance Agency for Higher Education.

QAA (Quality Assurance Agency) (2011a) *Code of Practice Chapter B11. Part B: Assuring and Enhancing Academic Quality Research Degrees* (Online). Available at: http://www.qaa.ac.uk/Publications/InformationAnd Guidance/Documents/B11.pdf (accessed 2 May 2014).

QAA (Quality Assurance Agency) (2011b) *Doctoral Degree Characteristics* (Online). Available at: http://www.qaa.ac.uk/Publications/InformationAnd Guidance/Documents/Doctoral_Characteristics.pdf (accessed 11 April 2014).

Race, P. (2007) *How to Get a Good Degree* (2nd edn) (Maidenhead: Open University Press Study Skills, McGraw Hill): 221.

Research Councils UK (RCUK) (2013) 'Pathways to Impact' (Online). Available from: http://www.rcuk.ac.uk/ke/impacts/ (accessed: 8 June 2014).

Rountree,K. and Laing, T. (1996) *Writing by Degrees: A Practical Guide to Writing Theses and Research Papers* (Auckland, NZ: Addison-Wesley/Longman).

Rudestam, K.E and Newton, R.R. (1992) *Surviving your Dissertation* (London: Sage).

Ruger, S. (2013) *How to Write a Good PhD Thesis and Survive the Viva*, Knowledge Media Institute (Milton Keynes: Open University).

Rugg, G. and Petre, M. (2004) *The Unwritten Rules of PhD Research* (Maidenhead: Open University Press).

Ryan, L. and Zimmerelli, L. (2006) *The Bedford Guide for Writing Tutors* (4th edn) (Boston, Bedford: St Martin's Press).

Sadler, D.R. (1992) 'Up the Publication Road: A Guide to Publishing in Scholarly Journals for Academics, Researchers and Graduate Students', *HERDSA Green Guide* (2nd edn).

Sandelowski, M., Voils, C.I. and Barroso, J. (2006) 'Defining and designing mixed research synthesis studies', *Research in Schools*, 13(1): 29–40.

Sankey, M. and St. Hill, R. (2009) 'The Ethics of Designing for Multimodality: Empowering Nontraditional Learners', in Demiray, U. and R.C. Sharma (eds), *Ethical Practices and Implications in Distance Learning* (Hershey: Information Science Reference): 125–54.

Schutz, P.A, Hong, J.Y, Cross, D.I, and Osbon, J.N. (2006) 'Reflections on investigating emotion in educational activity settings', *Educational Psychology Review*, 18(4): 343–60.

Seddon, T. (2010) 'Doctoral Education in Global Times: "Scholarly Quality" as Practical Ethics in Research', in Walker, M. and Thompson, P. (eds), *The Routledge Doctoral Supervisor's Companion* (London and New York: Routledge).

Shacham, M., and Od-Cohen, Y. (2009) 'Rethinking PhD learning incorporating communities of practice', *Innovations in Education and Teaching International*, 46(3): 279–92.

Slade, C. (2011).'Unlocking the doors to a doctorate', *The Australian*, 20 April·

Smith, M. and Deane, M. (2014) 'Supporting the neophyte writer: The importance of scaffolding the process', *Journal of Academic Writing*, 4(1): 40–51.

Smith, S. (2013) 'Moving towards an Interprofessional Education Programme For Students in Higher Education', PhD by Published Works, Leeds Metropolitan University.

Tate, S. (2004) 'Using Critical Reflection as a Teaching Tool', in Tate, S. and Sills, M. (eds), *The Development of Critical Reflection in the Health Professions*, Occasional Paper, no. 4.

Taylor, S. (2002) 'Managing Postgraduate Research Degrees', in Ketteridge, S., Marshall, S. and Fry, H. (eds), *The Effective Academic: A Handbook for Enhanced Academic Practice* (London: Kogan Page): 137.

Taylor, S. and Beasley, N. (2005) *A Handbook for Doctoral Supervisors* (Abingdon: Routledge).

Thomson, P. and Kamler, B. (2013) *Writing for Peer Reviewed Journals: Strategies for Getting Published* (London: Routledge).

Thomson Reuters, (1994) *The Thomson Scientific Impact Factor*, Thomson Reuters website (Online). Available at: http://thomsonreuters.com/business_units/scientific/free/essays/impactfactor/ (accessed 3 January 2014)

Trafford, V.N. and Leshem, S. (2002a) 'Starting at the end to undertake doctoral research: Predictable questions as stepping stones', *Higher Education Review*, 35(1): 31–49.

Trafford, V.N. and Leshem, S. (2002b) 'Anatomy of a doctoral viva', *Journal of Graduate Education*, 3(2): 33–40.

UKCGE (United Kingdom Council for Graduate Education) (1996) *The Award of a Degree of PhD on the Basis of Published Work in the UK* (Lichfield: UKCGE).

UKCGE (United Kingdom Council for Graduate Education) (1998) *The Status of Published Work in Submissions for Doctoral degrees in European Universities* (Lichfield: UKCGE).

UKCGE (United Kingdom Council for Graduate Education) (2004) *The Award of PhD by Published Work in the UK* (Lichfield: UKCGE).

Universities UK (2009) *Promoting the UK Doctorate: Opportunities and Challenges*. Research Report (London: Universities UK).

Watts, J.H. (2009) 'From professional to PhD student: Challenges of status transition', *Teaching in Higher Education*, 14: 687–91.

Watts, J.H. (2012) 'To publish or not to publish before submission? Considerations for doctoral students and supervisors', *Creative Education*, 3: 1101–10.

Wellington, J. (2010) 'Weaving the Threads of Doctoral Research Journeys', in Thomson, P. and Walker, M. (eds), *The Routledge Doctoral Student's Companion* (London and New York: Routledge): 128–42.

Wenger, E. (1998) *Communities of Practice* (Cambridge: Cambridge University Press).

Wenger, E. (2007) 'Communities of practice. A brief introduction', *Communities of Practice* (Online). Available at: http://www.ewenger.com/theory/ (accessed 11 January 2014).

Wenger, E. McDermott, R. and Snyder, W. (2002) *Cultivating Communities of Practice* (Boston: Harvard Business School).

West, M.A. (1994) *Effective Teamwork* (1st edn) (Leicester: British Psychological Society).

Williams, H. (2004) 'How to reply to referees' comments when submitting manuscripts for publication', *Journal of the American Academy of Dermatology*, 51(1): 79–83.

Willis, R. (2010) 'The alternative way to get a PhD', *The Independent*. (Online). Available at: http://www.independent.co.uk/student/postgraduate/postgraduate-study/the-alternative-way-to-get-a-phd-1942607.html (accessed at 8 June 2014).

Wilson, K. (2002) 'Quality assurance issues for a PhD by published work: A case study', *Quality Assurance in Education*, 10(2): 71–8.

Wisker, G. (2007) *The Postgraduate Research Handbook: Succeed with your MA, MPhil, EdD and PhD*, Palgrave Research Skills (Basingstoke: Palgrave Macmillan).

Wisker, G. and Robinson G. (2012) 'Picking up the pieces: Supervisors and doctoral "orphans"', *International Journal for Researcher Development*, 3(2): 139–53.

Woolf, S.H. (2008) 'The meaning of translational research and why it matters', *Journal of American Medical Association*, 299: 211–13.

Yates, l. (2010) 'Quality Agenda and Doctoral Work: The Tacit, the New Agendas, the Changing Contexts', in Thomson, P. and Walker, M. (eds) *The Routledge Doctoral Student's Companion* (London and New York: Routledge): 299–310.

Index